T0382251

52 AMAZING THINGS THAT BECAME TRUE OF YOU THE MOMENT YOU TRUSTED CHRIST

52 AMAZING THINGS THAT BECAME TRUE OF YOU THE MOMENT YOU TRUSTED CHRIST

STEPHEN KUHN

New York Boston Nashville

All emphasis (italics) in Scripture verses has been added by the author.

FaithWords Edition

Cover design by Steve Kuhn Design. Front cover type design by Brand Navigation.

FaithWords
Hachette Book Group
1290 Avenue of the Americas, New York, NY 10104
faithwords.com
twitter.com/faithwords

Originally published in 2015 by Belt of Truth Books in the United States.
First FaithWords Edition: April 2017

FaithWords is a division of Hachette Book Group, Inc. The FaithWords name and logo are trademarks of Hachette Book Group, Inc.

Library of Congress Cataloging-in-Publication Data has been applied for.

ISBNs: 978-1-4789-7073-6 (paper over board), 978-1-4789-7074-3 (ebook)

10 9 8 7 6 5 4 3 2 1

In memory of Paul Gossard.

You showed me what it looks like to trust God even in the midst of adversity.

You will be missed, my friend.

Contents

52 AMAZING THINGS THAT BECAME TRUE OF YOU THE MOMENT YOU TRUSTED CHRIST

Introduction

Who Do You Think You Are?

Who are you?

If you're anything like most people, your first response to that question is probably your job title. After that, you may list off your age, how many kids you have, or perhaps even your hobbies. If I'd been asked that question a few years back, I would have answered, "I am a graphic designer." This is true, but it's not really who I am—it's just what I do to pay the bills. I might also have told you that I am a dad to two of the coolest (and cutest) girls in the world, I'm husband to a wonderful and beautiful wife, I like being in the mountains, and I love bacon almost as much as I love air. Here's the deal, though—these things may *describe* me, but they don't *define* me. In order to figure out what defines you—your true identity—you need to understand who your Creator says you are. After all, He's the one who made you, so He is the only one with the authority to tell you what is true about you.

Who God Says You Are

As far as God is concerned, there are only two possible identities for every man, woman, and child alive today. You are either "in Adam"—the default state of all humans at birth—or, if you've trusted Jesus, you are "in Christ." You must be one or the other; you cannot be both. The most important thing to understand with regard to discovering what is true about you is understanding which camp you belong to.

You are no longer "in Adam"

The moment Adam chose to turn away from God, the cancer of sin entered into the human race and changed the default identity of everyone.[1] Since that day, every one of us has been born physically alive but spiritually dead:

> When Adam sinned, sin entered the world. Adam's sin brought death, so death spread to everyone, for everyone sinned (Romans 5:12).

Our identity at birth is now "in Adam," which means we're all born with a sin nature.

If you're a parent, it shouldn't be too hard to understand this. Unless your name is Mary, your sweet little kiddo didn't need to be taught how to sin. It's in their nature from day one to be selfish, to lie to you, to yell "NO!" when asked to do something they don't want to do. Did you ever sit down and

have a conversation with Junior discussing the benefits of dishonesty and how manipulation can be used for his gain? Of course not. Any child knows these things because they're born with a sin nature.

As long as your identity remains "in Adam," you are separated from God because of this sin nature within you. You are spiritually dead. You can do all sorts of good things here on earth, but ultimately none of them will matter in eternity because they will be done for your own benefit and not for God's glory. You are also forced to live your life, fight your temptations, and manage your pain using your own power. You're on your own. This does not mean God is not actively pursuing you while you remain "in Adam" (He certainly is), but ultimately you will need to reach out to Him and accept His help.

Don't be discouraged by this, though. If you are reading this book, there's a good chance your identity is no longer "in Adam." Why? Because the moment you placed your hope and trust in Jesus, your identity switched to "in Christ," and this separation no longer describes you!

You are "in Christ"

Just as everyone is born "in Adam," everyone is also given the opportunity to be born again "in Christ." The moment you place your hope and trust in Jesus to rescue you and set you free from your sinful nature, you are reborn with a new nature. Your identity is now "in Christ." This isn't a future reality that you must strive to achieve; it's bestowed upon you instantly. In other words, it's already done. Period. All that's left for you to do is believe it.

Chances are, you have a pretty good understanding that being "in Christ" means you are now reconciled to God. Even if you haven't spent much time in church, you're probably still familiar with John 3:16:

> This is how God loved the world: He gave his one and only Son, so that everyone who believes *in him* will not perish but have eternal life (John 3:16).

When we believe in Christ, we receive eternal life in heaven with God. Most churches do a wonderful job of preaching this central truth of salvation. What is sometimes missed, though, is the truth that this life "in Christ" is available to us right now! If we understand the Gospel as merely the promise of eternal life after death, we remain stuck trying to live life here on earth in our own power—living as if we are still "in Adam." We miss the reality that God has promised us His life (and all the benefits that come with it) today. It begins the moment our identity changes from "in Adam" to "in Christ."

Discovering What Is True About You Now That You Are in Christ

Throughout Scripture you will find many verses describing how you were changed the moment you placed your faith in Christ.

In this book, I've focused on 52 of these passages to help you understand more deeply what these truths mean for you personally. Some of these descriptions of who you are may not feel true about you, but I encourage you to trust and believe that they *are* true about you—because *all* Scripture is true, whether it feels like it is or not. The more you choose to trust them, the more your feelings will begin to align with Scripture.

Meditating on what God says is true about me has been deeply transformational in my life. It has been one of the key practices that set me free from addiction, freed me to love others more fully, and finally made my relationship with God feel real and intimate rather than merely ritualistic. For that reason, I believe this little book can have an equally large impact on your life as well.

So, let's find out who you *really* are...

1

Your Sins Are Forgiven

In Him we have redemption through His blood, the forgiveness of our trespasses, according to the riches of His grace.

EPHESIANS 1:7, NASB

One of my favorite weekend activities growing up was riding my bike to the local arcade and blowing my hard-earned paper route money on video games.

We had a few different arcades in town, but my favorite was the huge one inside the mall. This arcade was the first place to play the latest games, and it was the place you went to test your joystick skills against the best players in town.

But as much as I enjoyed beating other kids at *Street Fighter II*, my favorite activity was filling my pockets with prize tickets from the carnival-style games. I'd dump quarter after quarter into Skee-Ball, the creepy shoot-out-the-clown's-teeth-with-a-water-gun game, and of course, Whac-A-Mole.

The better you did at these games, the more tickets you earned. And the more tickets you earned, the more stuff you could buy from the prize counter.

These prizes ranged from single-ticket items like stickers

and tattoos all the way up to a full-on Sega Genesis console for some ridiculously huge quantity of tickets.

But what would have happened if I went to the counter and attempted to redeem real money for the Sega Genesis? I'd probably be told to come back when I had enough tickets—the only currency they accepted there.

In a lot of ways, we do the same thing when we look at the junk in our lives and attempt to overcome it by being a better person. We look at the debt of sin we've accrued and hope that by going to church, doing good works, or being a "nice enough person," we can tilt the scale back in our favor.

But that's not how forgiveness works in God's eyes. You may as well be trying to buy your way into heaven with arcade tickets.

The truth is, the only currency that can pay for your forgiveness is the blood of Jesus. It's His blood that has the power to redeem you and provides forgiveness for your sins—not your ability to be a good person.

This is great news, because once you realize your good behavior has nothing to do with you earning forgiveness, you can rest assured that bad behavior can never cause you to lose it.

Thankfully, God doesn't dole out His forgiveness the way an arcade game distributes tickets—in small batches and only if you win. He offers it to you solely as a gift of His grace.

Furthermore, He forgave all your sins the moment you put your trust in Christ.

You've been fully forgiven. You've been fully redeemed. Your debt has been paid.

So now, instead of trying to earn enough tickets to get to heaven by playing Whac-A-Mole with your sin, you can relax and join Jesus over at the air hockey table—knowing that even if you lose, you will still be loved unconditionally, forgiven completely, and accepted fully.

2

You Are Right with God

Therefore, since we have been made right in God's sight by faith, we have peace with God because of what Jesus Christ our Lord has done for us.

ROMANS 5:1

When the apostle Paul penned this verse, he had just finished writing an entire chapter explaining how Abraham was saved by his faith, not by his good deeds.

This must have been quite shocking to the original recipients of the letter because many of the Christians in Rome had grown up in the Jewish tradition. They saw Abraham as the father of their religion, which was based heavily upon following the rules to maintain a right standing with God.

But now Paul is telling them it wasn't actually Abraham's ability to be a good rule follower that saved him—it was his faith. Abraham trusted God, and that's the *only* reason God counted him as righteous.

Paul may as well have said up was down and down was up.

He could have stopped there, leaving Romans 4 as an

interesting biographical lesson on the life of Abraham, but thankfully Paul continued on to write the verse we're looking at today (and likely stunning his readers even more).

Paul wanted to make sure his readers knew that all these things he just told them about Abraham are also true for *everyone* whose faith has been placed in Christ. That includes you and me today.

In the same way Abraham's deeds had nothing to do with his righteousness, your deeds have no bearing on your righteousness either. Simply put, you can't earn God's acceptance through behavior.

At first glance, the idea that you could never do enough good to earn God's acceptance sounds like bad news, but actually it's wonderful news.

Think of it this way: If God's acceptance depended on your good works, how much good would you have to do to know that you'd earned it? At a minimum, you would need to do enough to compensate for your mistakes, right? And then, every time you messed up, you would have to do more good deeds to get back to the baseline.

I don't know about you, but that sounds exhausting. Plus, you would never know for sure whether you were doing enough, so you would always doubt God's acceptance of you.

But look once again at what Paul tells us in this verse. He makes it clear that we *have been* made right with God by faith.

Have been... Past tense. It's a done deal.

The righteousness you received had nothing to do with your good works then, and it still doesn't today.

By trusting that you have *already* been made right with God, it will free you from the endless treadmill of trying to earn your own righteousness.

And that, my friend, will lead you to tremendous peace.

3

You Are Loved with an Everlasting Love

I have loved you, my people, with an everlasting love.
With unfailing love I have drawn you to myself.
JEREMIAH 31:3

If you've ever seen the classic '70s film *Willy Wonka & the Chocolate Factory*, you will undoubtedly remember the scene where Wonka unveils his top-secret new creation: the Everlasting Gobstopper.

The Gobstopper, for those of you who didn't grow up pretending to be an Oompa Loompa, is a funky-looking jawbreaker that never gets any smaller. In the words of Willy Wonka, "You can suck them and suck them and suck them and they'll never get any smaller. Never!"

A single piece of this magic candy would last you the rest of your life because it would never diminish in size...never be reduced...never shrink in the slightest.

In other words, it would be *everlasting*.

ev·er·last·ing
adjective
Lasting forever; eternal: *everlasting future life.*

The Lord uses this same word when He describes His love through the prophet Jeremiah, which means *nothing* will ever make His love for you stop, shrink, or be reduced in any way.

The moment you put your faith in Christ, every barrier that ever stood between you and the everlasting love of God was removed forever:

- Your bad decisions will not reduce it.
- Your stubbornness cannot stop it.
- Your sin will never block it.

Or, to (loosely) paraphrase Willy Wonka, no matter how much you feel like you suck, God's love for you will never get any smaller.

4

You Are a New Creation

This means that anyone who belongs to Christ has become a new person. The old life is gone; a new life has begun!

2 CORINTHIANS 5:17

I don't know about you, but I've spent countless years of my life trying to make myself into a better person. My biggest struggle was always with pornography, and my typical approach to fixing it was a combination of willpower and filter software—neither of which worked for very long. I'd look at my addiction and think, *Life will only get better if I somehow fix this part of me.* Or worse, *God will only love me if I change.* Unfortunately, no matter what I did, I never could change for the better.[1]

Now this may surprise you, but since I've found freedom from porn, I've come to believe that God wasn't all that interested in changing me during those years of my addiction. Before anyone gets all spun up about that, let me explain what I mean.

I grew up in the church and trusted Christ very early in life. Which means, according to this verse, God had *already* changed me into a new person years before I ever got hooked on porn. But if that's truly the case, why did I struggle so much with sin (and, to be honest, still do at times)?

The answer, I believe, is that I'd never been taught the truth about how I had *already* been changed. I didn't realize that I had been given a *new* heart with *new* desires.[2] I didn't understand what it meant to have the Holy Spirit living inside of me, empowering me to resist temptation.[3] I had no idea that God had given me access to His wisdom and had already set me free from the power of sin.[4] I had all the tools and resources of the Kingdom available but never realized they were mine to use.

The question I should have been asking during the years of my addiction wasn't "What do I need to do to change myself for the better?" It should have been "How do I get to live my life now that God has already changed me?" Once I began focusing on what God had already done in me rather than what I could do for myself, I began to experience freedom from my addiction. Life was no longer about becoming someone new; it was about maturing into who God says I already am.

I'll be honest, though. There are still days where it doesn't feel like I've been changed. But I've discovered that whenever I wait for something to *feel* true before I'm willing to trust it, I might never experience it. However, if I choose to believe what God says is true about me regardless of whether it feels true, then the feelings inevitably come. Trusting that God has already changed me, regardless of my feelings, is what allows me to live my life as if He has.

In the same way, if you've trusted Christ, you can trust that God has already made you a new person as well. After all, that's what this whole book is about—learning to trust that everything God says has been done in you truly has been done in you.

So remember, God isn't interested in changing you.

Why?

Because He already has.

It's done.

5

You Have Become a Child of God

See how very much our Father loves us, for he calls us his children, and that is what we are!

1 JOHN 3:1

If you've spent much time around my blog,[1] you may wonder if it's more about being a father than finding freedom from pornography addiction. To be honest, there's a pretty good reason for that. The truth is, as much as I love writing about finding freedom from pornography, I simply can't help writing about being a dad. It's the greatest joy in my life.

The Bible refers to children as a gift from the Lord,[2] and even though there are days when I question how true that may be, I have to say I wholeheartedly agree.

I love my daughters more than anything. They are my joy. They are my blessing.

And you know what? My feelings toward them have nothing to do with their behavior or how "lovable" they are at any given moment. In fact, I remind them all the time that there is nothing they could do to make me love them any more or love them any less, because I already love them with *all* of my love, and that will never change.

I love them solely because they are my children.

But get this: The moment you trusted Christ, you became a child of God, which means the God who created the entire universe feels exactly the same about you!

You are God's joy.

You are God's blessing.

Even on your worst day, when you're wallowing in sin, throwing tantrums, and being a complete pill, God still looks at you and says, "Man, I love that kid. How lucky am I to have him as My son?"

God is absolutely crazy about you, and that will never change.

Why? Because you are now—and always will be—His child.

6

You Can Call God "Abba"

You have not received a spirit that makes you fearful slaves. Instead, you received God's Spirit when he adopted you as his own children. Now we call him, "Abba, Father."

ROMANS 8:15

I may be sacrificing any semblance of credibility for admitting this, but I absolutely love *Monty Python and the Holy Grail.* Yes, it's a ridiculous movie, and yes, it's not exactly the best theological commentary, but every time I watch it, I find myself laughing hysterically (and slightly ashamed at my ability to quote every line).

I particularly enjoy the scene where God sticks His head through the clouds and speaks directly to King Arthur. God is all business, and He appears to have become quite frustrated and impatient with humanity. At one point, He goes off on a tirade about how annoying His subjects are: "If it's one thing I can't stand, it's people groveling. Every time I try to talk to someone it's 'sorry this' and 'forgive me that' and 'I'm not worthy...'"

What stands out to me about this scene is how the filmmakers, in their attempt to create something humorous, have actually provided a sobering commentary on how many people truly do view God.

A lot of folks, when they think of God, see Him as a harsh cosmic judge or taskmaster. They see a man with a long beard and glowing crown (not unlike the picture of God presented in the movie), sitting on a throne bossing people around: "Do this, do that, follow the rules, and don't even think about doing anything fun or I shall smite thee!"

But that's not the picture of God we're given in the Bible. In fact, Paul tells us in Romans 8:15 that those who are in Christ don't need to fear God. The image of a cruel, impatient, and demanding God poking His head through the clouds to give us His marching orders is simply not true.

God doesn't see you as His slave; He sees you as His beloved child. He has adopted you into His family because He loves you with the perfect love of a sinless Father. This unconditional love is what allows us to respond to Him as our "Abba" (Daddy) and come to Him to be fathered rather than judged or condemned.

Imagine if King Arthur had addressed the movie version of God as "Daddy." I doubt He would have received a warm embrace. But that's the danger that comes with misunderstanding God's true nature: As long as you fear God's judgment, wrath, or condemnation as a slave driver, you will be more likely to grovel before Him than to run to Him for help whenever you fall.

But now that your union with Christ has made you a permanent member of God's family, there's no need to grovel. You can run straight to your Abba Father with confidence that He will embrace you no matter what.

7

You Have Been Set Free from All Condemnation

So now there is no condemnation
for those who belong to Christ Jesus.
ROMANS 8:1

If you've been around the church for a while, you've probably heard this verse a hundred times. But have you ever thought about what it actually means, particularly what it means for you?

For example, have you considered what percentage of your sin was paid for by Jesus at the cross? Was it 20 percent? 50 percent?

According to the Bible, it was 100 percent. *All* your sin was paid for at the cross.

Or, how much of your sin has been committed *after* Jesus paid for it on the cross?

Unless you're more than 2,000 years old, *all* of your sin has been committed after the cross.

It's probably easy for you to understand that every sinful thing you've ever done was paid for by Jesus, but do you realize that every sinful thing you have yet to do has already been paid for as well?

That's a difficult concept for our time-conscious minds to grasp.

Not for Jesus, though. When He died as the perfect sacrifice 2,000 years ago, He knew the entire list of sins you would commit over the course of your life (even those you will commit 10, 20, or 30 years from now), and His death covered every last one of them.

All the sins (past, present, and future) of all believers (past, present, and future) were paid for by His death.

It's this complete payment of all sin for all eternity that allowed Jesus to proclaim, "It is finished!"

No more guilt.

No more punishment.

No more condemnation.

None.

No matter how much you've sinned (or will sin), if your faith is in Christ, it's already been made right. No further justice or retribution will ever be required.

So from now on, when you sin, don't beat yourself up and feel as if your sin is causing God to see you as unacceptable. I would encourage you instead to come before God with thankfulness:

- Thank Him that Jesus already paid for the sin you just committed.

- Thank Him that He loves and accepts you unconditionally in spite of the sin you still commit.
- Thank Him that He only sees the righteousness of Christ in you no matter how many times you still mess up.

Odds are good that we all will continue to wrestle with sin in the years to come. But thanks to Jesus bending time and space to pay for our future sins with His past sacrifice, we can now run to God for grace and mercy rather than being fearful of His condemnation.

8

You Have Been Personally Chosen by God

Furthermore, because we are united with Christ, we have received an inheritance from God, for he chose us in advance, and he makes everything work out according to his plan.

EPHESIANS 1:11

I'm pretty sure I started bugging my parents for a dog right about the time I first learned how to talk. It was always made clear to me, however, that it just wasn't the right time for us to get one. I'd beg and plead to at least go and look at the pet store. They would give in, and then I'd inevitably fall in love with one of the dogs before being carried out sobbing.

After years of pleading, my parents finally agreed that it was time for us to get a dog. We decided on a breeder and then drove up to meet the puppies. The breeder pointed out the "perfect" pups and mentioned she would be keeping them for show dogs. We could have our pick of the others. We settled on a little female with one ear that stuck straight up and one ear that flopped over. This flaw may have rendered her "imperfect," but we still thought she was perfect for us.

The hardest part was even though we knew which puppy was ours, we still couldn't take her home yet. She was too young and needed to remain with her mother a while longer. During those weeks, I knew I had a dog; I just didn't have her with me yet. I'd resort to daydreaming about all the fun stuff we were going to do together and the tricks I'd teach her, and I kept getting more and more excited about bringing her home. By the time she did come home, I'd built up so much anticipation I could hardly bear it. Even though I'd only met her once and she hadn't done anything to earn my love, I couldn't wait for her to be united with our family.

When I think of how God has chosen me to become a part of His family, I'm sometimes tempted to believe there's no way He would have actually picked me if given the choice. I assume He *had* to let me in only because He was bound by His word. My logic goes something like this: God promises to receive anyone who trusts Jesus, and I've trusted Jesus. So, even though He probably doesn't like me and surely doesn't need me, He had no choice but to let me in lest He go back on His promise.

But that's not what the Bible tells us at all. The Bible makes it clear that God chose each one of us personally. Not to be His pets, but to be His adopted children, complete with full rights as His sons and daughters, even including an inheritance.

What's amazing to me is that He chose all of us *in advance*—even before we were united with Christ. It wouldn't surprise

me at all to find out God was thinking of you much the same way I was thinking of my dog before she was united with our family. I knew she was going to be mine; it was just a matter of time. And the longer I waited, the more excited I got for us to be together. God knew you were going to be His, and the longer He waited, the more excited He got about being with you.

The difference, though, is the only thing I could do was wait. God, however, was actively orchestrating the events of your life to lead you straight to Him. He knew how badly He wanted you specifically, so He did whatever it took to bring you home.

9

You Will Never Be Separated from God's Love

And I am convinced that nothing can ever separate us from God's love. Neither death nor life, neither angels nor demons, neither our fears for today nor our worries about tomorrow—not even the powers of hell can separate us from God's love. No power in the sky above or in the earth below—indeed, nothing in all creation will ever be able to separate us from the love of God that is revealed in Christ Jesus our Lord.

ROMANS 8:38–39

Chalk it up to my love of all things Middle Earth, but I can't read these verses without thinking of the *Lord of the Rings* movies. When I hear "No power in the sky...," I envision the Nazgûl swooping down on the backs of their fellbeasts to pick off the men of Gondor during their ill-fated retreat from Osgiliath.

"In the earth below..." brings to mind the fellowship's encounter with the fiery Balrog deep within the caverns of Moria.

And of course, "nothing in all creation" could include all the orcs, goblins, trolls, and the myriad other nasties found within Tolkien's world.

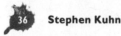

I picture those foul creatures and think of how lucky we are that these "powers" are only the stuff of fantasy.

Or are they?

Now, I'm not saying the Nazgûl are real, but it does sound like Paul wants us to recognize how sometimes the things we think of as fantasy are actually a very real (but unseen) part of our reality.

Angels...demons...powers of hell...

Paul is telling us that spiritual creatures do exist—and some of them are bent on your destruction. But his point isn't that you need to be afraid of them. In fact, quite the opposite.

Paul wants you to know that no matter what you come up against, nothing will ever be able to separate you from God's love.

Why? Because Christ has *already* sealed your destiny for all eternity. Which means that even death itself will be nothing more than your passage from this world into the loving arms of your Father.

So no matter what happens in your life from here on out, God will always love you just as much as He loves Jesus. And *nothing* will ever change that.

Not your secret sins.

Not the sins of others against you.

Not the mistakes from your past.

Not even the full power of hell set against you.

Nothing will ever separate you from the love of God because of what Christ has done for you.

10

You Became God's Masterpiece

We are God's masterpiece. He has created us anew in Christ Jesus, so we can do the good things he planned for us long ago.

EPHESIANS 2:10

A few days ago, after sharing this verse with my daughter, she asked me what a masterpiece was. Even though I'm an artist by trade, I still struggled to explain it in a way that a six-year-old would understand. What I eventually told her is that a masterpiece is an artist's favorite work. I asked her to think of all the drawings she had taped to the wall of her bedroom and to choose which one she was most proud of. Whichever one she picked was her masterpiece.

So how amazing is it that God, who created the entire universe—redwood forests, the Himalayas, snow leopards—still considers you and me to be His favorite works of art? I like to think that God's got pictures of us on His fridge, and whenever He invites the heavenly saints over for dinner, He points to my picture and says, *"Check out this kid! He was so messed up, but then My Son got ahold of him and now look at him. Talk about turning coal into a diamond. He turned out even better than I expected. He's one of My masterpieces!"*

Furthermore, it's important to remember that a masterpiece doesn't have to be a perfectly flawless work. I heard a fascinating story about an interaction between the great composer Igor Stravinsky and one of his best concert violinists that illustrates this idea wonderfully.

Stravinsky had just completed a piece that he considered to be his masterpiece. When it came time for the musicians to begin practicing the piece, the violin player became increasingly frustrated. No matter how hard he tried, he couldn't master it. It seemed impossible to get his fingers to move up and down the neck of his instrument in the manner and timing Stravinsky had dictated.

This man went up to the composer and humbly stated his concerns. "Mr. Stravinsky, the music is impossible to play. No matter how hard I try, I cannot do it perfectly. I fear I will ruin your masterpiece."

Stravinsky's response to him was unexpected. "I wrote your part knowing no one, not even the best violinist in the world, could ever play it perfectly. But I am not interested in perfect. I am interested in hearing the beauty of your *attempt* at perfection. That will lead to the most powerful music. That will make it a masterpiece."

My daughter's art isn't perfect, but I love it because she put her heart into it. The violinist couldn't play his piece perfectly, but Stravinsky loved his passion behind it. Your life is likely full of flaws, but God still loves you because you're exactly who He created you to be.

So, the next time you are feeling down on yourself, just imagine your picture on God's fridge. I bet you'll find it right next to mine.

11

You Are Welcome in God's Presence

Because of Christ and our faith in him, we can now come boldly and confidently into God's presence.

EPHESIANS 3:12

I don't know what it is about the waiting rooms in doctors' offices, but it seems they all come with a stack of outdated *People* magazines. Apparently, the best way to calm people's minds before their impending colonoscopy is to offer them reading material about the secret lives of celebrities.

As I thumbed through a few issues (you know... for science!), I got to see photos of George Clooney's fancy new estate on the Italian Riviera. Then there was an entire story updating everyone on the status of Kim Kardashian and Kanye West's marriage. And, of course, there were multiple pictures of celebrities doing such exciting things as grocery shopping and even walking along the beach with their kids.

None of these photos looked to be welcomed or endorsed by the celebrities. Rather, they were all taken from far away with a telephoto lens. In fact, some of these celebrities have made it quite clear that they don't want such intrusions into their private lives. According to the story about George Clooney, he made an agreement with the local police to fine anyone who ventures too close to his house with a camera. I think it's safe to say that most people are not welcome in the presence of famous people.

Now, I understand not wanting the paparazzi to follow you around spying on you everywhere you go. I'm not saying these celebrities are wrong at all for desiring to maintain some sort of private life in spite of the media intruding on them constantly. If someone started taking pictures of my family for TMZ, you can bet that I would surely respond the same way.

Imagine, though, if George Clooney and Kim Kardashian have such a problem with people trying to gain access to them that they need to separate themselves through legal boundaries, how much more attention does God receive from everyone trying to get to Him? You would think if anyone was going to wall themselves off from the hordes of fans and followers trying to get too close, it would be God.

In one sense, that *is* how it used to be. Prior to the cross, there was a thick curtain separating the room where God dwelled (the Holy of Holies) from the rest of the temple—and from the world. If anyone other than the high priest dared to go behind this curtain into God's presence, they would have died instantly. This was such a serious deal that even the high priest had to go through a ceremonial cleansing process to make sure his sins had all been removed before entering. In addition, the other priests would tie a bell and a rope around his ankle.

If the bell went silent, it meant the high priest had died and his corpse would need to be dragged out from behind the curtain. This may all seem harsh, but it's the reality of what happens to an unrighteous person who enters into the presence of God's holiness.

God, however, wanted to make a way for us to become welcome in His presence, and He had a plan to solve the problem. He sent Jesus to pay for our sins with His death, which immediately tore the temple curtain in two, proving to us that the separation is now gone. We've been invited into God's presence.

The moment you became unified with Christ, you were made holy and righteous because of your faith in Him. It's as if you were transformed into the same position as the high priest,[1] only now you've been purified *permanently*. You can be so sure of this that you don't even need to tie a bell on your ankle. Thanks to Jesus, you can now come into God's presence with boldness and confidence, any time you wish.

12

You Have Been Given Every Spiritual Blessing

All praise to God, the Father of our Lord Jesus Christ, who has blessed us with every spiritual blessing in the heavenly realms because we are united with Christ.

EPHESIANS 1:3

We have a general rule in our house that we're quick to share things with one another, but it's important to ask permission first. For example, anytime my daughter wants to play a game on my phone, she just needs to ask me before taking it. As long as there isn't a good reason for me to say no to her (such as unfinished homework or me expecting a call), I've promised to say yes whenever I can.

Now, imagine if my daughter kept asking permission to use my phone even after I handed it to her. She could be playing a game with the phone in her hands but still pop her head up every few minutes to ask if she can have the phone.

"Can I play a game on your phone?"

"You have my phone, honey."

"Can I play a game on your phone?"
"You still have my phone, honey."
"Can I play a game on your phone?"
"Really?"

Not only is that ridiculous, but it would be somewhat annoying as well. Probably on par with the never-ending "Are we there yet?" or "I'm huuuuuuungry."

Sometimes, though, I wonder if God looks at us and says, "Really?" when we keep asking Him for things that He's already given to us. After all, according to this verse, He's *already* blessed us with every spiritual blessing. But what exactly are these blessings? The remainder of this passage tells us more about them:

- You *have been* made holy (v. 4).
- You *have been* adopted as His child (v. 5).
- You *have been* offered His grace (v. 6).
- You *have been* redeemed and forgiven (v. 7).
- You *have been* given wisdom and insight (v. 8).
- You *have been* included in His inheritance (v. 11).
- You *have been* given the Holy Spirit (v. 13).

God has *already* given you these things, yet if you're anything like me, you keep coming back to Him asking for them again and again. That's why I try to pay attention to the language I use whenever I talk to God. Instead of asking to be forgiven when I mess up, I thank Him for how He has already

forgiven me. Instead of asking for His grace, I thank Him for the unending grace He's already showered upon me.

This may seem like nothing more than a subtle shift in semantics, but I've found it helps me remember that I don't need to strive to please God in order to receive His blessing. I've already received it. All I need to do is trust and believe that if God says it's true about all believers, it's true about me as well.

13

You Became Part of God's Royal Priesthood

You are royal priests, a holy nation, God's very own possession. As a result, you can show others the goodness of God, for he called you out of the darkness into his wonderful light.

I PETER 2:9

Imagine you're at your wedding standing across from the woman you love. The pastor is saying something about forever...rich or poor...better or worse...But if you're honest, it's all a blur. Your mind is fixated on the beauty in front of you.

You know you love this woman, and you decided long before this moment that you want to spend your life with her, so whatever you agree to at this point is just confirmation of what you already know in your heart.

The important thing to recognize is that this ceremony is the moment when you will finally become her husband.

For those of you who have been there, did you have any idea how to be a husband on the day of your wedding? Did you fully understand what you were agreeing to when you made those vows?

Nope. None of us did.

But that didn't change the fact that you still became a husband the moment you said "I do." It just means you now get to spend the rest of your life figuring out what being a husband looks like.

That's the thing about identity. You often become something long before you know how to actually be that something.

The moment you put your faith in Christ, you became a royal priest. You became holy. You are now possessed by God in the same way a husband and wife possess each other.[1]

Do you know how to be a priest? Do you know how to be holy? Probably not completely. But the more you trust that God has already made those descriptors true of you, the more you will learn how to live according to that truth.

You are already a priest. Now you can learn how to live as one.

You are already holy. Now you get to learn how to walk in holiness.

You are already God's possession, and not even death can separate the two of you.

As a result, "you can show others the goodness of God, for he called you out of the darkness into his wonderful light."

14

You Have Received Wisdom from God

God has united you with Christ Jesus. For our benefit God made him to be wisdom itself. Christ made us right with God; he made us pure and holy, and he freed us from sin.

1 CORINTHIANS 1:30

For the most part, school came fairly easily for me. I don't recall ever getting a poor grade on a test or paper unless I chose to blow it off (which is a whole 'nother story). As long as I paid attention and read my assignments, I could get a decent grade without having to put in too much effort.

For an overly imaginative and creative kid like me, this was both a blessing and a curse. Sure, I could breeze through my homework quicker than most kids, which was a good thing. But then what was I supposed to do with all my free time?

In my younger years, I would typically play with Legos, read Choose-Your-Own-Adventure books, or draw epic Ninja Turtles vs. *Star Wars* battles. As I got older, though, my decision-making skills seemed to regress.

Instead of building robots, I decided to stink-bomb the school cafeteria.

Instead of reading books, I chose to look at porn.

Instead of battling with action figures, I broke into cars for drug money.

The irony is, no matter how much trouble I got myself into, my grades never dropped. I remained on the honor roll at school despite all my poor decision-making.

I may have had a ton of knowledge, but I clearly didn't have enough wisdom.

Wisdom is defined as "the knowledge of what is true or right coupled with just judgment as to action."[1] You can know true facts about a million different things, but if you don't know how to apply that information to your life, it's just knowledge. Knowing facts and information may get you into the final round of *Jeopardy!*, but it won't help you navigate life unless you couple it with wisdom.

True wisdom, however, isn't something you generate on your own. As Paul shows us in this verse, the source of true wisdom is Jesus: "God made [Christ] to be wisdom itself."

Furthermore, God did this for *our* benefit. He knew that many of the decisions we would be faced with making in life would far exceed our pay grades. Which is why He made Christ to be the embodiment of wisdom, placed Him within us, and granted us full access to everything we will ever need to know.

As Charles Ellicott says in his *Commentary for English Readers*:

> Christ became to us God's revelation of Himself, thus giving us a wisdom from the source of all wisdom, which surpasses utterly any wisdom we could have derived from nature or from man.[2]

You can rest assured that God will never bring you to a tough decision only to leave you hanging. If you find yourself in a situation where you need wisdom, remember that wisdom itself already lives inside of you. All you need to do is ask for it.[3] He will make your path clear or give you the words to say.[4]

If there's one thing I've learned over the years, it's that God's wisdom far exceeds my own. Perhaps I'm wrong, but I have a feeling my decision to stink-bomb the school cafeteria wouldn't have seemed like such a great idea if I'd sought the Lord's counsel first.

But then again, if I had asked Him, I probably would have missed out on all those fun hours I spent staring at the wall of the detention room.

15

You Were Joined to the Lord

But the person who is joined to the Lord is one spirit with him.

1 CORINTHIANS 6:17

When I read about being one with the Lord in Spirit, I immediately think of the earthly example of this that God gives us in the Garden of Eden:

> That is why a man leaves his father and mother and is united to his wife, and they become one flesh (Genesis 2:24 NIV).

Yes, part of what this verse is talking about is the sexual union between a husband and wife, but it actually goes much, much deeper than that. As we see later when Jesus quotes this verse in His response to the Pharisees,[1] this union is the literal joining together of two individuals by God.

Two separate persons becoming one in spirit.

As I write this, it's been just over a week since my wedding. Needless to say, this idea of "two becoming one" has been on my mind a lot lately.

For the past year or so, I've been falling more and more in love with the woman who has now become my wife. During that time, I desired to learn everything I could about her, discover what makes her happy and learn to avoid doing anything that might make her question why she keeps hanging out with me. I wanted to be with her as much as I could. Even if we were doing nothing together, at least we were *together*.

As great as this was, at the end of each day she would go back to her house or I would go back to mine, we deposited our paychecks into separate accounts, and we didn't even have the same last name.

We were together, but we had not yet become *one*.

Today, however, thanks to the covenant of marriage, we are one. We now share the same house, the same bank account, and the same last name. Deeper than that, though, our souls have been joined together by God. We have become one in spirit.

Yes, we are still two distinct individuals, but from here on out, we will always be one entity: "the Kuhns."

The same is true with you and Jesus.

There may have been a period before you trusted Christ when you were interested in finding out more about Him—a time when you wished to discover if He truly was who He said He was.

Or perhaps you spent many years trying to impress Him with behavior and sacrifices in order to feel closer to Him. (That was my story.)

If you've never made the commitment of trusting Him

as your Savior, though, you've only been courting Him. You're still going home to separate houses each night.

If, however, you have trusted Jesus with your life, then you've *already* become one with Him in spirit.

Your eternity has been fully aligned with His eternity.

Your debts were completely satisfied when He added His signature to your spiritual bank account.

Even your heavenly name has been changed[2] to reflect who you are now that you're in permanent union with Christ.

Everything changed for me the moment I pledged myself to my wife on our wedding day and the two of us became one in God's eyes. But as wonderful as this has been for us, it is nothing compared to the eternal union we've received with our Lord and Savior.

And being able to know that we've been made one in spirit with the Lord, well, *that* is truly something worth celebrating.

16

You Are No Longer a Slave—You Are a Friend of Jesus

I no longer call you slaves, because a master doesn't confide in his slaves. Now you are my friends, since I have told you everything the Father told me.

JOHN 15:15

Back in the early 1800s, deep within the American South, some folks in a small town were getting ready for an event that was taking place that afternoon. This wasn't a typical event like a carnival or a wedding. No, these folks were setting up for a slave auction.

As hard as it is to look back at the reality of something as shameful as a slave auction, at this time they were still lively affairs—at least for those who were only there to observe. Many of the townsfolk would come to watch the wealthy plantation owners arrive in their fancy coaches and bid on new workers for their growing operations. The work on these plantations was physically demanding, so the strongest and most muscular slaves would fetch top dollar.

Elijah, however, was not one of these powerful men. He was a small boy who was sure to be overlooked by the majority of the bidders. He knew before he even stepped in front of the crowd that he would likely be purchased by one of the smaller farms—if he was purchased at all.

Elijah was understandably frightened as he was forced onto the bidding stage.

The auctioneer held his arm out toward Elijah and shouted, "Do I hear a dollar for this…this…runt of a boy?"

The crowd jeered with laughter.

"I need something to replace my mousing cat," shouted a man in the front. "I'll pay a dollar."

"I need someone to clean up under my horses. He's just the right size! I'll pay two!" another man yelled.

As the auction progressed, the bidding climbed slowly but still remained far below the price of a typical slave. Elijah became more and more embarrassed as the crowd continued to belittle him.

He was ashamed.

He felt worthless.

The life of a slave was horrible enough, but adding public ridicule was almost too much. Elijah wished this life of torment forced upon him would somehow end.

But then a man from the back stepped forward. "I will pay the highest price for this young man. I see value in him that none of you see, and I must have him as my own."

Everyone, including Elijah, was shocked. But the man was indeed serious, and he took Elijah home with him that day for a sum far exceeding what anyone had expected.

As soon as they arrived at the man's sprawling estate, Elijah

asked him what his first job would be. He knew there would be nothing but endless work for him on a plantation as large as this man's.

"No, Elijah. I did not purchase you to extend your slavery. I purchased you to set you free. From now on, you will live not as my slave, but as my son—and as my friend."

•••

You and I may never have suffered the cruel fate of slavery in the American South, but we all were slaves to something far more sinister.

Every one of us was born under slavery to sin.[1] And if we wanted to overcome this sin, we became slaves to the law.[2] We had to strive endlessly toward reaching a point of perfection—a job that none of us could ever fulfill. We were like the young Elijah, unequipped for the demands forced on us, facing a future without any hope of freedom.

Thankfully, God loves you far too much to leave you hopeless. He bought your freedom, knowing that you would never be able to pay for your own release from slavery. He paid your ransom—at the unthinkable cost of His Son's blood—to purchase back the right to your soul for eternity.

Now, because you are set free in Christ, you are no longer a slave.

You are no longer bound by the impossible yoke of a cruel taskmaster.

You are God's friend, and He has set you free.

17

You Have Been Adopted by God

To all who believed him and accepted him, he gave the right to become children of God.

JOHN 1:12

You know what's absolutely amazing? The God of the universe, Creator of Earth, the One who holds everything together, has adopted you as His child.

Think about that for a second and just try to comprehend what it means.

If you're a parent, consider how much you love your kids. As much as you love them, though, it's with an imperfect, human love.

God loves you even more than you love your kids, because He loves you with His holy, unconditional, and righteous God-love.

Jesus tells us an amazing story of God the Father's love in the parable of the lost son.[1] In the story, a rebellious son demands his inheritance from his father immediately. Culturally, this was the same as telling his father, "You're dead to me now." But rather than yelling at his son or punishing him, the father gives his son the money, lets him leave, and waits in anticipation for his return.

Every day the father looks off into the distance, hoping to see his son returning. When the son finally does return, the father doesn't even give his boy a chance to grovel. He runs to him with open arms and tackle-hugs him at full speed! No matter how much the boy rejected or disobeyed his dad, there was nothing he could have done to make his father stop loving him.

Do you realize this is actually a story about God's love for you? No matter how much you've messed up, He will always be standing there with His arms wide open—just like the father in the story—waiting for you to come home to Him. It doesn't matter what you've done or where you've been. None of it will make any difference in how much He loves you.

I never understood the depth of a love like this until my daughters were born. I can say without a doubt that there is nothing my girls could ever do to make me stop loving them. No matter how many times they hit me as toddlers, yell at me as teenagers, or disown me as adults, I will always be there waiting for them with open arms. I simply cannot fathom living my life apart from my favorite girls no matter what they do. Honestly. I'm even getting a bit choked up now just typing these words and thinking about how much I love them.

But as much as my daughters mean to me, you mean even more to God as His adopted child.

He loves you to the same extent that He loves Jesus.

18

You Will Never Be Abandoned by God

Do not be afraid or discouraged, for the Lord will personally go ahead of you. He will be with you; he will neither fail you nor abandon you.

DEUTERONOMY 31:8

Did you know the most common command the Lord gives us in the Bible is "Do not fear"?

Why is that? Perhaps it's because He knows us well enough to know that our natural tendency is to be afraid:

- Afraid our needs won't be met.
- Afraid our life won't turn out how we hoped.
- Afraid the people we love will abandon or reject us.

More often than not, these fears are rooted in a lack of trust. They are the result of not trusting that *everything* God says applies to those who are in Christ *is* true—even for you.

You see, when you put your trust fully in the Lord, you will come to see how His promises overcome all of your fears.

After all:

What does Matthew say about God meeting your needs?

Don't worry about these things, saying, "What will we eat? What will we drink? What will we wear?" These things dominate the thoughts of unbelievers, but your heavenly Father already knows all your needs. Seek the Kingdom of God above all else, and live righteously, and he will give you everything you need.

So don't worry about tomorrow, for tomorrow will bring its own worries. Today's trouble is enough for today (Matthew 6:31–34).

What does Jeremiah say about God's plans for your life?

"For I know the plans I have for you," says the Lord. "They are plans for good and not for disaster, to give you a future and a hope. In those days when you pray, I will listen. If you look for me wholeheartedly, you will find me" (Jeremiah 29:11–13).

What does today's verse in Deuteronomy say about God abandoning you?

Do not be afraid or discouraged, for the Lord will personally go ahead of you. He will be with you; he will neither fail you nor abandon you (Deuteronomy 31:8).

The more you trust the love of Christ, the less you will need to be afraid.

This is how trusting that God is always right there with you, that He will never fail you, and that He will never abandon you—no matter what—sets you free from fear.

19

You Have Been Washed Clean

"Come now, let's settle this," says the Lord.
"Though your sins are like scarlet,
I will make them as white as snow.
Though they are red like crimson,
I will make them as white as wool."
ISAIAH 1:18

Sin. You probably don't need me to tell you it's an issue in your life. After all, we all struggle with it. Every one of us.[1]

No matter how good we try to be, we've all been soiled by the stains of our sin.

When Isaiah wrote these words, he was looking forward to the day when these stains on our souls would be taken care of. When we could finally be cleansed from our sin—permanently.

But he also recognized that we could never make ourselves clean on our own. He knew that no amount of scrubbing, hiding, or justifying would remove the scars of sin from our souls.

Isaiah understood that only Jesus had the power to make us clean.

And today, thanks to His finished work on the cross, He has.

You see, the moment you placed your trust in Christ, your sins were washed as white as snow.

Not by anything you did.

Not by your striving toward goodness.

Not by your ability to overcome your flaws.

It was solely by the power of Christ's blood.

And nothing will ever change this. No sin—not even the sin you have yet to commit—will ever leave a stain on you again.

Because, as the Lord says in today's verse—it's already been settled.

20

You Have Been Given the Confidence to Be Bold

Since this new way gives us such confidence, we can be very bold.
2 CORINTHIANS 3:12

Boldness. Confidence. Bravery. Chutzpah.

Whatever you call it, it's the same idea: the ability to face fear, danger, or opposition—all for the name of Christ.

Is boldness something you generate on your own? Can you just "man up," "grow a pair," and overcome whatever fears are holding you back from proclaiming the love of Christ to others?

Maybe for a bit, sure. But not consistently. At least not to the level it will take to reach the far corners of the earth.

For that, it will take the confidence that only comes from understanding this "new way" Jesus has brought us into:

> The old way, with laws etched in stone, led to death, though it began with such glory that the people of Israel could not bear to look at Moses' face...Shouldn't we expect far greater glory under the new way, now

> that the Holy Spirit is giving life? If the old way, which brings condemnation, was glorious, how much more glorious is the new way, which makes us right with God (2 Corinthians 3:7–9)!

The old way—following the rules and making sacrifices—led to death. Why? Because we couldn't follow the rules. No matter how hard anyone tried to be good enough, they knew deep down they were failing.

Sure, they could make sacrifices to temporarily cover the death penalty for their sins, but what if they missed one? There was constant fear that some sin was left unaccounted for. No one could truly know for sure if they were right with God. They had no confidence because their hope was tied to their own abilities.

But now that you are in Christ, you have been brought into the "new way." You have been made right with God because of what Jesus has done for you—not because of what you tried to do for Him.

In addition, you now have the Holy Spirit living within you, empowering you with the same eternal life that brought Jesus back from death.

And the best part is, this righteousness, power, and life will last forever. You cannot lose it. It will never be taken away from you. Which is why you can trust this new way with an everlasting confidence, empowering you to boldly proclaim its good news to everyone who has yet to hear it.

21

You Are Delighted in by God

For the Lord your God is living among you.
He is a mighty savior.
He will take delight in you with gladness.
With his love, he will calm all your fears.
He will rejoice over you with joyful songs.
ZEPHANIAH 3:17

I love my daughter.

Yeah, I know, she's my kid, so I kinda *have* to love her, right?

But I genuinely love her. I'm crazy about her. In fact, I'd rather spend time with her than anyone else. You might even say I *delight* in her.

Last weekend, we celebrated my birthday. And like any 34-year-old, I rented a bounce castle for the afternoon.

Did I actually want a bounce castle for my birthday?

Well, yeah, I kinda did.

But what I wanted even more was to see the smile on my daughter's face as the castle began to inflate and take its shape. I wanted to hear her laughter and shouts of joy as we bounced for hours.

I delight in my daughter's happiness because I delight in her. Her joy is my joy.

In the same way, God delights in you as His adopted child. And sometimes He chooses to bless you for no other reason than to delight in your joy with you.

He did that for me at my party last Saturday. When all the kids ran inside to gorge themselves on cupcakes, I stayed back to lie down in the middle of my little inflatable kingdom and rest for a few minutes. In that moment, engulfed in the warm sunshine and inflated vinyl, I sensed the Lord speaking to me:

> "I gave you this sunshine as a gift to show you My love. The angels and I are having a great time up here watching you kids have fun. Happy birthday, My son. You are My joy. I delight in you. Don't ever forget it."

22

You Have the Holy Spirit Living in You

Don't you realize that your body is the temple of the Holy Spirit, who lives in you and was given to you by God?

1 CORINTHIANS 6:19

Did you know there is a difference between the *laws* of the Old Testament and the *commissions* of the New Testament epistles?

The laws of the Old Testament are telling us, "You must do this or else there will be punishment." The commissions of the New Testament are telling us, "Because of the power of Christ within you, this is how you get to act now."

See the difference?

The New Testament isn't a bunch of additional rules and commands telling us how to live a good life for Jesus. It's telling us who we are now that we are in Christ. The New Testament is telling us what it will look like when we let Jesus live His life through us.

Any time you find what appears to be a command in the New Testament epistles, look for an "in Christ" statement nearby. I've found it's always close by. For example, look at the following verse from Paul's letter to the church in Corinth:

> Run from sexual sin! No other sin so clearly affects the body as this one does. For sexual immorality is a sin against your own body (1 Corinthians 6:18).

How many times have you read that as a command telling you to resist sexual temptation by your own power…or else? But look at the verse immediately following:

> Don't you realize that your body is the temple of the Holy Spirit, who lives in you and was given to you by God (1 Corinthians 6:19)?

Paul knew the church in Corinth hadn't fallen back into sexual immorality because they were too weak to resist temptation. It was because they had forgotten who they were in Christ. They forgot they had the power of the Holy Spirit living within them.

Instead of telling them to shape up and knock off their bad behavior, Paul simply reminds them to remember who they are now that they are in Christ.

Likewise, if you are struggling with sexual immorality (or any sin, really), it's not because you are still a slave to sin; it's because you have forgotten who you are in Christ. If you can remember that the Holy Spirit now lives within you, you can rely on Him to give you the power to honor God with your body.

23

You Have Become a Member of Christ's Body

All of you together are Christ's body, and each of you is a part of it.

I CORINTHIANS 12:27

I'm convinced the 1980s were the golden decade for cartoons. Feel free to argue with me on that, but you probably won't change my mind. Now, I can admit that my opinion may be tainted by personal nostalgia, but you have to admit there were some pretty awesome classics back then.

My personal favorite, hands down, was *Voltron*. Five kids, each with their own giant robotic lion, who would combine together to form the massive robot, Voltron. Every episode followed the same basic template—a bad guy shows up, the kids try to battle him as individual lions, realize they're overmatched, and then combine forces as Voltron to save the day.

This same basic template has shown up in multiple cartoon series even to this day. *Transformers* (a close second to *Voltron* in my mind) had multiple iterations of these "combiners": Devastator (formed from the five Constructicons), Defensor (formed from the five Protectobots), and the impressive Predaking (formed from the five Predacons). Even the long-running *Power Rangers* series with their "Megazord" was clearly inspired by (i.e., ripped off) the *Voltron* template as well.

If there's one thing I've realized over the years, it's that these shows I loved so deeply as a boy spoke to me for a reason. More often than not, it's because they awakened something inside of me that God had put there intentionally. In the case of *Voltron*, it's this idea that we're all given an important role to play as part of a larger team—God's team.

The moment you trusted Jesus, you became part of the body of Christ. You may not have received a giant robotic lion, but you were made into the hands and feet of Jesus. In other words, He wants to use you as the instrument through which He does good works in this world and for you to be His tangible representation to everyone you meet.

Practically speaking, this means that instead of merely praying for peace in the world and wondering why God isn't answering that prayer, perhaps you should consider whether He's put that particular desire on your heart because He's chosen *you* to do something about it. Maybe He wants to use you as His arms to deliver a loving embrace to your city or family.

I can tell you one thing for sure—God didn't save you so you could just sit there in your robotic lion and watch '80s cartoons while the body of Christ functions without you. Anytime Voltron went into battle even one lion short, it didn't go

well—not until everyone was able to contribute and the body was whole once again.

Luckily, the body of Christ doesn't have any paralyzed limbs either. As long as you show up, you'll be given all the power and energy you will need to do whatever He calls you to do. Your life now flows from the same source that's been empowering countless generations of believers to change the world through His love.

So don't settle for being a mere spectator. As a member of Christ's body, you're now part of the team. You may be the green lion, or perhaps you're the red one. Either way, the body can't function as well without you.

24

You Have Been Cleansed and Made Holy

Some of you were once like that. But you were cleansed; you were made holy; you were made right with God by calling on the name of the Lord Jesus Christ and by the Spirit of our God.

1 CORINTHIANS 6:11

The most important thing in life, hands down, is to figure out how to be made right with God. If your life on earth comes to an end before that is taken care of, you will be separated from Him for all eternity.

That, my friend, is bad news.

What are we to do, then? Well, step one is to recognize and acknowledge that this separation between you and your Creator exists. But after that, then what?

Many people reach this point and conclude they must try harder, do better, buck up, and follow the rules as best they can. Ideally, at the end of their life, they will have done more good than bad (or at least more good than most other people), and then God will welcome them into heaven.

This is, in essence, what all religion teaches: Be a good person and you might get to go to a better place when you die. But the problem with this is, we can't do it. We can't become good people, at least not on our own.

Sure, you may consider yourself to be a good person, but are you perfect? Are you holy? Because the gap that exists between man and God can only be overcome if man is somehow made holy. And man, left to his own devices, can never become holy.

This is why Jesus is so much better than religion.

God knew man couldn't clean himself up. He knew man couldn't overcome the separation that existed between them. Yet God loves every single one of us so much He was willing to do whatever it took to remove the separation from us—even if it cost Him the life of His son.

And it did.

When you called on the name of Christ and reached out to Him to save you, Jesus made you clean. It had nothing to do with your ability to clean yourself up, follow the rules, or become a good person.

Jesus made you holy.

Jesus made you right with God.

It was all because of Jesus.

That, my friend, is good news.

25

You Have the Ability to Be Thankful in All Circumstances

Be thankful in all circumstances, for this is God's will for you who belong to Christ Jesus.

I THESSALONIANS 5:18

What words stand out the most to you in this verse?

Thankful?

God's will?

What about the one word most of us tend to miss: *all*? Because you are in Christ, you can be thankful in all circumstances.

Sure, it's easy to be thankful for the *good things* that come along in life:

- You landed a new job. Schweet!
- The doctor just told you the cancer is gone. Thank You, Jesus!

But what about the hard things?

- You just got fired…
- Your teenage son got his girlfriend pregnant…
- Your wife served you divorce papers…

Crickets.

As much as we want to ignore it, that one little word is still there. Be thankful in *all* circumstances—the good ones…and the bad ones.

But how in the world can God expect us to be thankful when the crap hits the fan in our lives? It's because He knows that He can make all things work together for your good.[1]

When you trust that God really can (and will) use *all* things—even the bad things—to bring you to a better place, it gives you hope, increases your faith, and allows you to respond with thankfulness.

Yes, it sucks that my addiction resulted in the end of my first marriage. But God used that bomb in my life to bring me face-to-face with my own brokenness. The pain of my divorce, along with the realization that my sin had caused it, was what finally allowed me to recognize my need for a Savior.

If it weren't for that "bad situation," I don't think I would know Jesus today in the way that I do. I would still be looking at porn, hurting my wife, and desperately trying to control my life.

As crazy as it seems, I am thankful for the path my life has taken—even for my divorce.

So the next time something bad happens in your life, remember that God has promised to make good come from it. You may not know how right away. You might not even get the answer this side of heaven. But God has promised you that He will. So if nothing else, you can be thankful for the fact that God will always keep His promises.

26

You Have Become an Ambassador of Reconciliation

For God was in Christ, reconciling the world to himself, no longer counting people's sins against them. And he gave us this wonderful message of reconciliation. So we are Christ's ambassadors; God is making his appeal through us. We speak for Christ when we plead, "Come back to God!"

2 CORINTHIANS 5:19–20

What if I told you God didn't just save you *from* something but that He saved you *to* something?

You see, God's purpose for sending Christ to die for you goes much deeper than only saving *you* from death. His plan has always been to recruit this new you as a fully alive, redeemed, hope-filled messenger of reconciliation to those who remain lost.

In other words, God has called you to be His ambassador.

According to dictionary.com, an ambassador is "a diplomatic official of the highest rank, sent by one sovereign or state to another as its resident representative." In plain English, an ambassador is a messenger sent from one kingdom to another. And not just any messenger, but one who has been trusted by the highest ranks with the most important and sensitive information. If you're negotiating with a foreign dignitary on behalf of the president, you probably aren't going to do it through e-mail. You would send an ambassador to talk with him or her face-to-face.

Furthermore, you would want to make sure the person you sent as your ambassador understood the local customs, spoke the language, and ideally had an established relationship with whomever you were sending them to communicate with. This is why official U.S. ambassadors typically live within the country they've been assigned to. They are not citizens of that country, but they've chosen to live their lives there in order to develop relationships and become more effective in their communication.

So, what does this lesson in foreign relations have to do with you and me?

God's plan is to recruit you (as well as all believers) to represent Him and share the news of His Kingdom with those who remain separated from Him. That's why He doesn't just zap us into heaven the moment we believe, and why it's probably not the best idea to hide yourself in an underground bunker lest you be tempted by negative influences. You're called to enter into the world of those around you (as much as you can without grieving the Holy Spirit), develop friendships with them, and share the love of Christ abundantly. Ideally, through these relationships, opportunities for deeper discussion will arise naturally, allowing you to share the story of how God has reconciled you back to Himself—an offer that is available to all.

Even if you're just beginning your journey to freedom, you can still tell others of the ways Jesus has already changed your life. Please don't buy the lie that you need to "arrive" at some point of perfection before your story is worthy of being told. The only thing required of you to be an ambassador of Christ is to simply be *in Christ.*

27

Your Sin Debt Was Paid in Full by Jesus

For God made Christ, who never sinned, to be the offering for our sin, so that we could be made right with God through Christ.

2 CORINTHIANS 5:21

Imagine you receive a letter in the mail one day. As you read it, you realize you've been found guilty of tax evasion. Not only that, but it's also been going on for years.

Because of back taxes and fines, you now owe the IRS over $500,000! Your entire net worth is pennies compared to the fine. You can barely make a dent in it, and can never, ever pay the complete fine.

In addition, the minimum prison sentence is 20 years.

You show up at the trial and realize there is substantial evidence against you. Financial records, invoices, previous tax returns—it's all there. You have no case.

You plead with the judge, claiming it was an accident and you honestly had no idea you were doing anything wrong. He sternly reminds you that ignorance is no excuse for criminal behavior. You broke the law and now you must pay the consequence.

The gavel slams against the bench as he sentences you to the maximum prison term in addition to your fine.

As you're being escorted out of the courtroom, however, the judge speaks up:

> "Stop! You may not know this yet, but I love you more than you can fathom. I can't bear to see you punished like this. I will have my own son pay your fine. He will serve your sentence for you. I can transfer all of your guilt to him, allowing you to go free as one who is forgiven and restored to righteousness. You must decide, though, if you trust him to do this for you. Will you receive this gift of forgiveness?"

You ponder the offer for a moment. It seems too good to be true. But then again, you have no other options. You're desperate. It's too late for you to undo what you've already done.

> "Yes, Your Honor. I trust your son. I need him to save me since I will never be able to overcome my own guilt."

Immediately, the handcuffs are taken off you and placed upon the wrists of the son.

You are now free.

Your debt has been paid.

As the son is escorted out of the room, you thank him with tears in your eyes. You have never felt such an overwhelming sense of relief—or gratitude.

Friends, this is not just a story. This is the Gospel.

This is what Jesus did for you the moment you trusted Him: He took your guilt, trading you His righteousness in return.

28

You Have Been Seated in the Heavenly Realms

[God] raised us from the dead along with Christ
and seated us with him in the heavenly realms
because we are united with Christ Jesus.
EPHESIANS 2:6

There seems to be a lot of talk in churches these days about believers being crucified with Christ. That's a good thing, of course, because it's true.[1] But what I don't hear as much is how those who've trusted Christ have been raised up from death with Him as well.

It's almost like we're hearing only the first half of the Gospel.

Paul reminds us of that sometimes-forgotten second half of the Gospel in Ephesians 2:6: the reality that *everything* God did for Jesus (including raising Him from the dead and seating Him in heaven), He did for you as well because of your unification with Christ.

This means you were not only connected to Jesus in His death, but you were connected to Him in His resurrection and ascension as well.

Your soul *already* has eternal life and *already* lives in heaven.

This concept can be hard for us to wrap our brains around. After all, if you're reading this, you're still living with a physical body. Every day you will touch, feel, smell, and taste things from the world around you. Your physical reality is likely to feel much more real to you because you're constantly experiencing it in tangible ways.

All of which can make it that much harder to grasp this idea that your soul—the truest, deepest part of who you are, the part of you that will live for eternity—is already seated in heaven (no longer here on earth).

Someday, your body will shut down for good. At that point, you'll be given a new body and your physical and spiritual realities will merge together for the rest of eternity. But until then, I find it helpful to remember it this way: Everything that happened to Jesus *physically* has already happened to you *spiritually*.

- Jesus was crucified *physically*; you were crucified with Him *spiritually*.
- Jesus was resurrected *physically*; you were resurrected with Him *spiritually*.
- Jesus is currently present in heaven *physically*; you are currently present in heaven *spiritually*.

But what's the point of all of this?

I find this truth to be most helpful on those days when it's difficult to face the broken reality of this world. Whether it's the constant evil I hear about in the news or pain and heartache present in my own life—trusting that my soul is seated in heaven next to my Savior helps me to not lose hope.

I receive great peace through knowing that no matter what happens to me here on earth, my eternity in heaven with Jesus is eternally secure.

And how can I know that?

Because I'm already there.

29

You Have Been Rescued from Darkness

He has rescued us from the kingdom of darkness and transferred us into the Kingdom of his dear Son, who purchased our freedom and forgave our sins.
COLOSSIANS 1:13–14

There's a recurring theme you may have noticed in many of the stories and movies we've grown up with. It's the idea that life appears to be wonderful and happy, and then one day the character's eyes are opened to an evil they've never noticed before.

We see this theme in the *Lord of the Rings* when the hobbits go about their laid-back lives in the Shire completely unaware of the growing darkness surrounding them. It's the central element of most fairy tales: an innocent child/princess/critter finds themselves mixed up with an evil witch/wolf/giant and then suddenly singing sonnets with birds and squirrels has to take a backseat to survival. We even see this theme in the great twentieth-century cinematic masterpiece *Dumb and Dumber*, when Harry and Lloyd set off on a happy-go-lucky cross-country adventure completely oblivious that they've become wrapped up in a criminal hostage situation.

Inevitably, these stories all end with a triumphant rescue. Sauron and his armies are defeated and peace is restored when the true king returns to his throne. Snow White is awoken from her poison-induced slumber by the prince. The FBI shows up to arrest the bad guys just as Harry and Lloyd are about to be shot. Darkness is overcome, life can return to the way it should be, and the hobbits can go back to eating second breakfast in peace. Like most themes we see repeated throughout popular stories, this one appears so frequently because it speaks to what we all know on some level to be true: There is darkness in this world, and we need to be rescued from it.

Everywhere you look today you see pain and suffering. If you need a reminder of this fact, just turn on the evening news. It's not hard to recognize how this world we live in truly is a kingdom of darkness. But it's also important to realize that this world is not what you and I were created for. We were created to be with our God "in the Kingdom of his dear Son." According to the apostle Paul, God has *already* rescued us from the kingdom of darkness. He purchased our freedom and forgave our sins through the work of Jesus, clearing the way for us to be transferred to God's Kingdom—the Kingdom we *were* created for.

I believe this transfer is one of the reasons the darkness in this world continues to break our hearts so deeply. Now that we are no longer part of that system, we have the ability to stand back and see it for what it truly is. This clarity of perspective has opened our eyes to the true source of the darkness—sin—and made us aware of how many people are still trapped by it. Knowing, however, that our eternity is secure in the Kingdom of God's dear Son, we now have the freedom to be courageous as we aid in God's continued rescue of those who remain lost. We may still be scarred by the darkness in this world, but it will never again enslave us. We, my friends, have been set free from that kingdom.

30

You Have Been Given the Incomparable Riches of God's Grace

God can point to us in all future ages as examples of the incredible wealth of his grace and kindness toward us, as shown in all he has done for us who are united with Christ Jesus.

EPHESIANS 2:7

Now that my daughter is getting a bit older, I decided it was finally time to introduce her to the world of Harry Potter. Ideally, this would have been done through the books, but since I only have her for short periods of time each week, we chose to watch the movies instead.

At the beginning of the first film, *Harry Potter and the Sorcerer's Stone*, Harry doesn't know the truth about himself, and much of the movie is dedicated to him discovering that he's actually a powerful wizard. This has been true about him all along, but it had been hidden from him. Without knowing his true identity, he believed the false description of himself he'd received from his abusive foster parents—that he was unwanted, unloved, and a worthless nuisance.

In one of the scenes where Harry begins to discover the truth, we see him shopping for all the supplies he will need as a student. He asks Hagrid, the giant-man who has come to take Harry to wizard school, how in the world he's supposed to pay for all the required items. Hagrid responds by casually telling Harry not to worry about all that. In the next scene, we see Harry's face begin to glow as the door to his family's vault swings open. It's full of gold coins—more than Harry will ever need—and it all belongs to him.

As I watched this scene, I was reminded of how we as believers have already received the incredible wealth of God's grace and kindness. How many of us, though, have lived much of our lives unaware of the treasure we've been given? Much like Harry, we still believe we're penniless beggars relying on the generosity of others to meet our daily needs. In reality, we have been given the key to heaven's vault and received full access to God's grace for our lives today.

But that's not really the main idea of this verse. Ephesians 2:7 is telling us that God's main purpose for showering us with His grace and kindness wasn't for our glory—it was for His. He did it, in today's language, to show off.

I like to think this is already playing out in heaven today. I imagine the angels looking down as they watch mankind destroy our own lives and the lives of those around us, which would lead them to question how anyone could see anything worth saving in humanity. But then I imagine God responding, "Just wait. You'll see. When the time comes and heaven is full of My redeemed saints, you will understand. My grace and kindness will never be more apparent to you—or to all of creation—than it will be on that day."

Our salvation will be a shining example for all eternity of how vast and powerful God's grace and kindness truly are.

31

You Have Been Filled with God's Light

Once you were full of darkness, but now you have light from the Lord. So live as people of light!

EPHESIANS 5:8

Have you ever tried to stop light from spreading?

Perhaps you've put your hand over a flashlight in a dark room, but the light still spilled out around your fingers, causing them to glow pink in the thinner spots.

You could always try putting a bucket over the flashlight, but would the light really be gone? Not at all. The inside of that bucket would still be lit up even if you couldn't see it from the outside.

The light of Christ has this same effect within you. You used to be full of darkness, but now that you are in Christ, His light is illuminating your heart and giving life to your soul. Whether you can see it or not, it's there. And nothing will ever be able to shut it off.

However, just like the flashlight, it's up to you whether you share it with others. You can keep it hidden, or you can allow it to shine on those around you. Jesus made it pretty clear what He is hoping you will choose:

> No one lights a lamp and then puts it under a basket. Instead, a lamp is placed on a stand, where it gives light to everyone in the house. In the same way, let your good deeds shine out for all to see, so that everyone will praise your heavenly Father (Matthew 5:15–16).

So don't hide God's light. Let it shine! Love others with the love of Christ. Offer the same grace and forgiveness that He offered you.

Be a beacon of hope for those who are still wandering in the darkness.

After all, isn't that what it means to live as people of light?

32

You Have Been Set Free from Fear

God has not given us a spirit of fear and timidity, but of power, love, and self-discipline.

2 TIMOTHY 1:7

What's your biggest fear? Snakes? Planes? Snakes on a plane? Regardless of what it is, every one of us is afraid of something.

According to a quick Google search, the top ten fears of people are:

- speaking before a group;
- heights;
- insects and bugs;
- financial problems;
- deep water;
- sickness;
- death;
- flying;
- loneliness; and
- dogs.

Chances are, you can relate to at least one of these.

If there's one fear on this list I relate to, it's probably the fear of loneliness. Before I remarried, I sometimes wondered if God's plan for my life included me remaining single indefinitely, which caused me to fear the loneliness that I assumed would come with long-term singleness.

But, remember, God has not given me a spirit of fear, which means I no longer had anything to truly be fearful about. Nonetheless, this fear of singleness remained a part of my life. So what gives?

In order to understand this dichotomy, we need to recognize that there are two types of fear:

- Legitimate fear (fear of a very real and present danger)
- Illegitimate fear (fear of an imagined or assumed danger)

When fear sneaks back into our lives as believers, it's *always* illegitimate fear. It's fear that is not based on the truth. Ultimately, it's a sign that we don't believe God will keep His word.

Let's look at that top-ten list again. How many of those fears are still legitimate once we hold them up to the truth of Scripture?

Do we still need to fear financial ruin if we recognize that God has promised to meet all our needs?[1]

Do we need to be afraid of death (which is ultimately what the fear of heights, deep water, and many other fears are about) if we understand that death doesn't separate us from God but releases us into glorious eternity with Him?[2]

Once we recognize how Jesus has set us free from any legitimate reason to be afraid, our fears are all exposed as illegitimate.

As I placed my focus back on the truth of God's love for me, I recognized that I wasn't actually lonely, even in my singleness. The love I received from my friends, my family, and from God Himself was more than enough to satisfy my heart's desire for companionship. And the same can be true for you as well.

So the next time you're afraid, look to the Scriptures and see what God says about whatever is frightening you. Perhaps you will discover that, thanks to the Spirit of Christ within you, you no longer have anything to truly be afraid of.

33

You Have Received Power, Love, and Self-Discipline

God has not given us a spirit of fear and timidity, but of power, love, and self-discipline.

2 TIMOTHY 1:7

In the last chapter, we looked at the first half of this verse and saw how God has not given us a spirit of fear and timidity.

In this chapter, we get to look at what He *has* given us: a spirit of power, love, and self-discipline.

First, those who are in Christ receive His power. No, this doesn't mean you'll instantly add 100 pounds to your squat the minute you hand your life over to Jesus. But it does mean you now have the power of Christ within you, equipping and enabling you to do whatever He calls you to do.

The best part about Christ's power at work in you is that you no longer need to rely on your own power, which, if you're being honest, is extremely limited. The power of Christ, however, is infinite.

Second, those who are in Christ receive His love. We are told that we love because He first loved us.[1] In other words, unless we first experience the love of Christ, we cannot effectively love others. We must receive it before we can offer it.

Sure, you can try to love others, but there will always be at least a small amount of self-interest driving your motivation. Under the surface, your love will be given with the hope of receiving their love in return. (Not that there is anything wrong with receiving love. The problem is when your offer of love is *conditional* upon being loved in return.)

However, once you trust that the unconditional love of Christ applies to you, it frees you from needing to obtain validation from others. Your need for love will be fully met by Christ, and only then can you offer love to others completely free from any external motivation.

Finally, those who are in Christ are given a spirit of self-discipline. We often look at following Jesus as an outside-in process: *If I change my behavior, my heart will become alive to Christ.* In reality, following Jesus is an inside-out process: *If I submit my life to Christ, He will redeem my heart and give me a new nature.*

The message of Christ isn't "Become a better person so I can love you." No, the message of Christ is "You can't become a better person on your own, but because I love you, I will make you a new person even in spite of your brokenness."

We have power because *His* spirit of power empowers us.

We can love others because *His* spirit of love dwells in us.

We can resist temptation because He has given us *His* spirit of self-discipline.

So the next time you feel you need more power, more love, or more self-discipline, don't look to your own ability to drum it up. Recognize that the Spirit of Christ dwells in you, so you already have all the power, love, and self-discipline you will ever need. Instead of trying to generate more of these things, I encourage you to trust that you already have more than you will ever need.[2]

34

You Have Been Brought Near to God

But now you have been united with Christ Jesus. Once you were far away from God, but now you have been brought near to him through the blood of Christ.

EPHESIANS 2:13

If I were to ask you to name the TV show you watched more than any other as a child, there's a good chance you would say *Sesame Street.* It's been on the air since the 1960s and broadcasted in more than 120 countries, so odds are you're familiar with it even if you grew up outside of the United States.

I don't remember a whole lot from the show, but one segment has remained cemented in my mind for over 30 years now: the one where the furry blue Grover monster was determined to teach us the difference between *near* and *far.*

The sketch begins with Grover standing right in front of the camera. "Near!" he proclaims boldly. He then proceeds to run quite a few paces backward, his Muppet arms flailing about humorously as he yells "FAR!" loud enough for us to still hear him. This shtick goes back and forth a dozen or so times as Grover becomes more and more exhausted trying to communicate his point. As a finale, he collapses in dramatic fashion, which of course is pure comedy gold to a four-year-old.

Yes, this may just be a silly sketch meant to teach children about "near" and "far," but it's also a good illustration of how we as believers can burn ourselves out trying to get closer to God through our own effort.

Remember, every one of us was born separated from God because of our sin. In other words, we were "far" away from Him. Many of us, myself included, tried to close this distance by being a good person, trying really hard to please God, and relying on our own abilities to run closer to Him. But our unification with God was never meant to work that way, so no matter how hard any of us tried, we could never get closer to God through human striving. The only thing our efforts could produce was exhaustion.

But now that you are in Christ, that devastating reality no longer applies to you! You may have come into this world far from God, but He wanted you close to Him. That's why He sent Jesus to cover the penalty for your sin with His blood. It was Christ who brought you near to God.

You could have spent your entire life running, trying to save yourself, but it never would have brought you any closer to God. But now, you finally get to stop running, because you're *already* where you're supposed to be.

35

You Became a Citizen of Heaven

We are citizens of heaven, where the Lord Jesus Christ lives. And we are eagerly waiting for him to return as our Savior.

PHILIPPIANS 3:20

I've been fascinated with Arnold Schwarzenegger since I first watched him star in all those cheesy '80s action movies. His entire life story, from coming to America as a bodybuilder to becoming governor of California, sounds as if it had been written by Hollywood screenwriters. It seems like everything he ever wanted to experience he found a way to make happen—no matter how grandiose it seemed at the time.

Needless to say, when his autobiography, *Total Recall*, came out, I was super excited to read it. One of the things that fascinated me the most in his story was how meaningful it was for him to finally gain U.S. citizenship:

> As long as I live, I will never forget that day 21 years ago when I raised my hand and took the oath of citizenship. Do you know how proud I was? I was so proud

that I walked around with an American flag around my shoulders all day long.

Arnold had won the Mr. Olympia competition a record-setting seven times, starred in major blockbuster movies, and built a fortune as a real-estate mogul. Yet even with all of those experiences, one of the proudest moments of his life was the day he finally became a citizen of the United States of America.

For someone like me who was born in America, I don't spend a lot of time considering what my citizenship means for me. I've been entitled to all the rights, privileges, and benefits that come from being an American my entire life. I've never known any other way. For someone like Arnold, however, they've experienced what it's like to be on the outside looking in. They've known what it's like to live in other countries—for better or worse—or to live within the United States as a noncitizen.

The moment someone gains U.S. citizenship, they instantly receive all the rights that come with that. In Arnold's case, he now could vote in U.S. elections, receive access to public benefits, and hold certain government jobs (such as governor). In addition, any children he had as a U.S. citizen (or any children he adopted from a foreign country) would be considered full U.S. citizens as well.

In the same way, the moment you put your faith in Christ, God adopts you as His child. You become a citizen of heaven, instantly receiving all the rights, privileges, and benefits that come with it. Your *earthly* citizenship may still be in America,

France, Nigeria, or some other country, but your *eternal* citizenship will forever be in God's Kingdom.

On that day when you finally reach the gates of heaven, God will look at your passport, see that Jesus has already stamped it, and say to you, "Welcome home, child."

36

You Can Now Do Everything God Calls You to Do

I can do everything through Christ, who gives me strength.

PHILIPPIANS 4:13

I used to be a distance runner...until one of my knees blew up.

Anytime I felt like stopping halfway into a run, I'd think about this verse and push forward. After all, the verse says that I can do *everything*, so surely that must mean I can finish a ten-mile run, right?

If you approach the verse with that logic, though, it can get a bit silly.

- If a 10-mile run qualifies, wouldn't a 1,000-mile run also fall under the category of *everything*?
- Does the power of Christ within my skinny, 170-pound body empower me to be an NFL lineman?
- Can I join the professional bull riders' circuit with no prior experience?

See what I mean? Silly.

When you read this verse in context, however, you realize that the apostle Paul is actually talking about enduring the difficulties that can come from following Christ. He's telling us that we can trust God to give us the strength to handle everything He calls us to do—even when faced with opposition.

No, the power of Christ within you probably won't enable you to bench-press a Buick, but it will enable you to offer love to your enemies...to forgive those who persecute you...to give joyfully and sacrificially...to trust God with your entire life.

After all, none of us are capable of doing *any* of those things on our own.

But remember, God never expected you to do them on your own. He intends for you to do them by trusting the power of Christ, which you were given the moment you believed.

37

You Have Received All the Riches You Need

This same God who takes care of me will supply all your needs from His glorious riches, which have been given to us in Christ Jesus.

PHILIPPIANS 4:19

Isn't it fun to daydream about what you would do if you won the lottery?

Every time I drive by one of those billboards advertising the current multimillion-dollar jackpot, I definitely give it some thought. I'd like to think that I'd give most of the money away and use it to bless others, but I know I'd spend at least some of it on myself. For example, I'd sign up to climb Mount Kilimanjaro, I'd order an Electric DeLorean, and I'd buy the giant marquee sign from the Kuhn Cinema in Lebanon, Oregon (after all, that is my last name).

Do you realize, though, that the moment you trusted Christ, you already won the lottery? Actually, what you received far exceeds any earthly payout of riches, because your riches in Christ are all based in heaven. Unlike the riches of this life that will rot away (I can't take my DeLorean to heaven, for example), these riches are eternal.

God has promised that His riches will meet all of your needs—every last one of them. If you trust God to keep His word in this area and allow that truth to penetrate your heart, it will save you untold amounts of worrying.

Now, I'm not saying God is a big slot machine who wants to make you rich and famous. His promise is to meet your needs, not your wants. I wish the Bible promised me a DeLorean, but I just can't find that verse in there no matter how hard I try. Probably because I don't actually *need* a DeLorean. In fact, earthly riches can be quite effective at keeping you distracted from what you truly do need. Just ask the rich man from the Lazarus parable.[1]

What I truly need—what we all need—is Jesus.

And if that need isn't met, nothing else matters.

38

You Have Been Set Free from the Law

Christ has truly set us free. Now make sure that you stay free, and don't get tied up again in slavery to the law.

GALATIANS 5:1

For years, I had accepted the fact that Jesus paid for my sins on the cross, but every time I messed up, I felt the need to earn God's favor back and ask forgiveness for what I had just done.

I believed that my initial salvation came from the work of Jesus alone (saved by grace), but I also believed my continued salvation—and my acceptance by God—was a reward I maintained only if I was somehow good enough (saved by keeping the law).

I kept going back to the slavery of the law even though Christ had set me free from it.

But remember: When did Jesus pay for your sins? It was on the cross.

And how many of your sins were committed after the cross? All of them.

Every one of your sins—past, present, and even future sins—were paid for 2,000 years ago when Jesus said, “It is finished.”

When you accepted Christ’s payment for your sins, it was for *all* of them. Not just the ones you had committed up to the point of your initial salvation.

This idea that we need to keep coming back for forgiveness and make things right every time we sin is the same as telling Jesus we need Him to go back to the cross and do it again.

It’s telling Jesus that what He did wasn’t enough.

This is why it is so important to understand how your behavior—no matter how sinful it may be—can never separate you from God’s love or acceptance once you have put your hope in the work of Christ.

Remember, Jesus is your *only* hope of freedom.

The minute you put your faith in Him, your debt was paid in full.

You were set free from the treadmill of trying to do enough good to overcome the inevitable junk that remains.

Trust this truth, and you will remain free.

39

You Have Been Made Complete

So you also are complete through your union with Christ, who is the head over every ruler and authority.

COLOSSIANS 2:10

I can remember the feeling of something missing from my life as far back as my early teen years. As I grew older and my hormones began to take over, I began to believe that missing piece would be found in relationships. All I needed to do was find a girlfriend and then I would be happy. She would complete me.

Somehow, around my sophomore year of high school, I finally convinced a girl to date me. I'd developed an interest in girls long before that, of course, but all my previous attempts at charming them had failed miserably.

But now that I had a girlfriend, why did the hole remain? Surely it must have been her inability to meet my needs—or so I believed.

Inevitably, we broke up and I began a decade-long cycle of moving from relationship to relationship, hoping to find the right girl who could fill that void and complete me. But no girl ever did, because the hole in my soul was never meant to be filled through human relationships.

Yes, relationships are important. They can be a source of happiness, joy, and love in your life. But they can't—and won't—complete you.

Only Christ can truly complete you and make you whole. And the best part is, if you are in Christ, He already has.

When you were united with Christ, He filled that hole in your heart. Which means you don't have to keep searching for the missing piece to your puzzle. You can finally be done looking for the right person, the perfect job, or whatever else you currently believe will fill the void and make your life complete.

You already are complete, because Christ has made you complete!

40

Your Roots Have Been Planted in Fertile Soil

Let your roots grow down into him, and let your lives be built on him. Then your faith will grow strong in the truth you were taught, and you will overflow with thankfulness.

COLOSSIANS 2:7

Jesus once told a story about a farmer who was planting seeds.[1] Some of these seeds fell on the hard path and were quickly eaten by birds. Some fell on shallow soil and appeared to grow just fine, but as soon as the hot sun came out, they withered and died. A few of the seeds fell into the thorns and were choked out by the more aggressive plants.

Wow. Thanks for the bummer story, Jesus.

Yes, if the story had stopped there, it would be a total downer. Thankfully, the story doesn't stop there.

Jesus tells us about a fourth group of seeds that landed in good soil. Fertile, life-giving soil, full of nutrients and moist with the water of life. These seeds not only grew, but they also produced crops that were up to 100 times more than what was planted!

What we often fail to realize, however, is this story isn't

really about how to plant seeds. It's about the condition of your heart:

> The seed that fell on good soil represents those who truly hear and understand God's word and produce a harvest of thirty, sixty, or even a hundred times as much as had been planted (Matthew 13:23)!

The moment you put your faith in Christ, the soil of your heart was transformed into rich, fertile soil because of His presence within you! Which means you *already* have everything you need to establish deep roots that drink from the water of life. Not because you're a special seed (sorry), but because your roots have been planted in Christ.

41

You Have Been Identified as God's Own

[God] has identified us as his own by placing the Holy Spirit in our hearts as the first installment that guarantees everything he has promised us.

2 CORINTHIANS 1:22

One of my earliest experiences with an installment plan was back in the mid-'90s when I purchased my first car—a pistachio-green 1976 AMC Pacer.

Oh man, it was a thing of beauty.

Actually, it was probably one of the most hideous cars on the road at the time. But I didn't care. I had a vision for what it could be.

I had saved up some money from my paper route, but not enough to fully cover the $1,500 it would take to make it mine. So, like many kids, I took out a loan from my parents.

We agreed that I would pay them back in installments until the loan was fully satisfied. The cool thing was they still let me put my name on the title. If I'd taken out a loan from a bank, the bank would have kept the title until it was paid in full. My parents, however, gave me full rights as the owner of my car even though I still owed them money on it.

From the very first installment, the Pacer was legally mine.

Knowing the car belonged to me, regardless of whatever condition it was in, made me love it unconditionally. I invested countless hours into sanding and repainting it, reupholstering the interior, and fixing the myriad mechanical issues that were inevitable with a 20-year-old engine. If the car had belonged to someone else, there's no way I would have put the time, money, or effort into transforming it into everything I'd pictured it to be.

In the same way, the moment you trusted Christ, God signed His name on the title of your soul by giving you the Holy Spirit. Your heart is in His name now, and no one else will ever repossess it.

Furthermore, because you belong to God, you can be sure that He will fulfill everything He has promised to do in you. You may still feel like an old beater at times—peeling paint, broken transmission, flat tires—but God sees your full potential. He can't wait to get you into His shop to restore you into the classic car that you are.

Yes, it will take time, and the job will never be fully complete this side of heaven. But that doesn't mean God will love you any less in the meantime.

I loved my Pacer when it was pistachio-green just as much as I loved it the day I drove it home from the shop with a fresh coat of paint and shiny new chrome rims.

Why? Because the Pacer was mine.

And you, my friend, are God's.

42

You Have Been Given Assurance that You Will Rise from the Dead

For since we believe that Jesus died and was raised to life again, we also believe that when Jesus returns, God will bring back with him the believers who have died.

I THESSALONIANS 4:14

What if I told you zombies were real?

Now, don't go running off to buy a chainsaw or a shotgun just yet. This verse doesn't mean you need to worry about brain-eating zombies crawling out of their graves and chasing you into a pub.

In order for us to understand what's really going on here, we need to look at the broader context of this passage:

> We tell you this directly from the Lord: We who are still living when the Lord returns will not meet him ahead of those who have died. For the Lord himself will come down from heaven with a commanding shout, with the voice of the archangel, and with the trumpet call of God. First, the believers who have died will rise from

> their graves. Then, together with them, we who are still alive and remain on the earth will be caught up in the clouds to meet the Lord in the air. Then we will be with the Lord forever. So encourage each other with these words (1 Thessalonians 4:15–18).

When we read this passage in context, we can see that Paul isn't talking about the dead coming back to steal life away from those who are still living (zombies); he is talking about Christ coming back to restore life to those who are already physically dead (resurrection)!

You see, the early believers in Thessalonica were concerned that anyone who believed in Christ but died before His return would miss out on the resurrection and eternal life. Which is why Paul encourages them to rest in the truth of what God has promised us will happen when Christ returns:

- Those who have died after trusting in Christ will be resurrected first.
- Living believers will follow closely behind.
- All believers will be reunited with their loved ones.
- All who are in Christ will be reunited with God!

So yes, my friend, the dead will rise. But they won't be zombies; they will be resurrected children of God!

43

You Have Received the Gifts of Faith

Oh, how generous and gracious our Lord was! He filled me with the faith and love that come from Christ Jesus.

1 TIMOTHY 1:14

Have you ever thought, *I just need to generate more faith*?

I know I have.

But here's the deal. Faith isn't something you can increase on your own; it's a gift from God.[1]

When a man brought his son to Jesus and asked for him to be healed, Jesus asked if he truly believed in his heart that what he was asking for could be done. In other words, did he have faith?

And how did the man respond?

> Immediately the boy's father cried out and said, "I do believe; help my unbelief" (Mark 9:24).

This man had heard about Jesus healing others, so he believed *in his head* that what he was asking for could be done. But that isn't faith…it's knowledge. Faith is when your belief moves from your head into your heart.

For this man, faith came the moment he believed the healing he had seen Jesus offer to others was available to him as well. And in order to believe that, he needed Jesus to help him overcome his unbelief.

Did Jesus respond to this man's request with a list of things for him to do to increase his faith? Not at all. Jesus healed the man's son, proving His faithfulness *in spite of* the man's unbelief.

Jesus knew that only His faithfulness would increase the man's faith.

Every time you choose to trust Jesus, He will come through for you. Always. And the more He proves to be faithful, the more your faith will increase. Looking at it that way, it's easy to see how faith is not something you generate on your own; it's the result of Jesus coming through for you 100 percent of the time.

44

Your Value Has Been Confirmed by God

God bought you with a high price.

1 CORINTHIANS 6:20

I'm not typically one to get excited about reality TV, but I'll admit I can watch *Pawn Stars* for hours. There's just something fascinating about seeing the random stuff people bring in, and even more so seeing them haggle about what it's worth.

For example, one guy brought in a box full of sunken treasure. Full-on rupees that had rusted together after being at the bottom of the sea for a hundred years or so. As it turns out, they were authentic and (supposedly) worth over $700,000.

Or, on the other end of the spectrum, one kid brought in a pair of 20-year-old Air Jordan shoes in mint condition expecting to get a few hundred bucks out of them. After a bit of investigation, they ended up being rerelease throwbacks from 2009. Final value: $75—about $50 less than what they retailed for originally.

What makes this show so much fun is the fact that you never

know who's going to come through the door and what they're going to sell. Even the people bringing things in often have no idea what their item is actually worth.

Now, imagine if someone brought *you* in as their item to sell at the pawnshop. How would that conversation go? For me, I expect it would go something like this:

Seller: I've got a standard-issue Oregonian native, probably made sometime around the early '80s. He's in decent shape other than starting to show some wear spots on the top of his head.

Buyer: Interesting. What were you hoping to get for him?

Seller: I was thinking $200.

Buyer: I don't know, man. We see a lot of these. Plus, look here: He's clearly got some issues. I see signs of some messed-up junk in his past, so there's probably some baggage from that. And see that...the guy has some lingering issues with selfishness and pride. You'd think by this age those would have worn off of him, but apparently not this guy. The best I can do is $10.

After all, isn't that what these guys do? They point out every flaw and look for any reason they can find to haggle the price lower. They're not interested in confirming the item's value. They only want to reduce how much they need to pay for it.

Aren't you glad God doesn't look at us that way? This verse in 1 Corinthians reminds us of how God would respond if someone offered to sell you to Him: He'd buy you without question. Not only that, but He'd also pay the highest price for you, fully confirming your worth and value.

How can we know that's what He would do?

Because that's exactly what He already did.

So the next time you feel flawed or worthless or wonder if you even matter to God, remember how valuable you truly are: valuable enough that God bought you from the enemy at the cost of His Son's life.

45

You Have Received the Promise of Life

I [Paul] have been sent out to tell others about the life he has promised through faith in Christ Jesus.

2 TIMOTHY 1:1

The apostle Paul knew his calling was to tell others about the life that is promised to those who trust Jesus. But what exactly is Paul talking about when he says "life"?

The way I look at it, there are two possible ways to interpret Paul's use of the word *life* in this context. On one hand, we could read this as Paul saying, "Here's what your day-to-day life will look like if you choose to follow Jesus." If this were the message God wanted to communicate to the world through a man, though, don't you think He would have chosen someone other than Paul?

Seriously, take a look at Paul's life:

> I have worked harder, been put in prison more often, been whipped times without number, and faced death

> again and again. Five different times the Jewish leaders gave me thirty-nine lashes. Three times I was beaten with rods. Once I was stoned. Three times I was shipwrecked. Once I spent a whole night and a day adrift at sea. I have traveled on many long journeys. I have faced danger from rivers and from robbers. I have faced danger from my own people, the Jews, as well as from the Gentiles. I have faced danger in the cities, in the deserts, and on the seas. And I have faced danger from men who claim to be believers but are not. I have worked hard and long, enduring many sleepless nights. I have been hungry and thirsty and have often gone without food. I have shivered in the cold, without enough clothing to keep me warm (2 Corinthians 11:23–27).

Prison…beating…shipwrecks…sleeplessness. I'm pretty sure nobody is going to voluntarily sign up for a life like Paul's—not unless there's something attached to it so amazing that it makes all these hardships pale in comparison.

Ah, but there is something attached to it: the life of Christ living within you. *Eternal life.*

This is the life that Paul is talking about.

You see, Paul's calling wasn't to tell others how Jesus wanted to change their day-to-day lives. His calling was to help them see their need for the eternal life of Christ to redeem their hearts (which would give them the power to thrive within their day-to-day lives).

Hopefully you won't ever find yourself shipwrecked or starving, but if you do, rest in the fact that the same life of Christ that dwelled in Paul dwells in you as well.

Which means when your day-to-day life gets hard, you can do more than simply try to survive... you can thrive.

46

You Have Been Granted Full Access to God

Let us come boldly to the throne of our gracious God. There we will receive his mercy, and we will find grace to help us when we need it most.

HEBREWS 4:16

As a child of God, you have full access to God whenever you want. You can come before God and ask Him to help you with your struggles, give you His strength to make it through a difficult circumstance, or even give you His wisdom in a specific situation.

You can come before Him and ask Him *anything*.

Not only that, but also God actually *wants* you to come before Him with your needs and desires. He honestly cares about whatever is on your mind:

> Give all your worries and cares to God, for he cares about you (1 Peter 5:7).

Think of it this way: How hard is it to be granted an audience with the president of the United States? Apparently, there isn't even a clear path laid out for the average citizen to meet the president. The closest I could find was a page on the presidential website allowing you to enter a drawing to hopefully win an invitation to a dinner with him—but it expired six years ago. That leaves me the option of performing some amazing act of heroism that will gain me national attention or winning the Super Bowl (I think those guys usually get a White House invitation).

But what if the president was my dad?

Do the president's kids need to enter a contest to win dinner with their daddy? Nope. They can walk into the Oval Office and hang out with him pretty much whenever they want.

As a child of God, you've got the same level of access to Him as the president's kids have to their dad.

So come before God and let Him know what's on your heart. He won't reject you or push you away. He will accept you fully as His child, showering you with His unending mercy and grace.

47

You Have Been Given Assurance of Eternity in Heaven

And this is the secret: Christ lives in you. This gives you assurance of sharing his glory.

COLOSSIANS 1:27

Want to know the secret to never doubting your salvation? It's simple: The presence of Jesus living within you gives you assurance of sharing in God's eternal glory. This means your salvation doesn't depend on anything you do or anything you don't do. It's all because of what Jesus has done for you.

This is great news because it means you can't screw it up!

In order to fully grasp what this means, we should look at the complete definition of *assurance*:

as•sur•ance [uh-shur-uhns]

noun

1. a positive declaration intended to give confidence.
2. promise or pledge; guaranty; surety.
3. full confidence; freedom from doubt; certainty.

The presence of Christ within you gives you confidence that your eternity will be spent living in glory. It's a promise from God, guaranteed to never change, setting you free from any doubt or uncertainty regarding your salvation!

As long as you're looking at salvation as a reward for you being a good person, you will always question whether you've been good enough. If, however, you trust that the work of Jesus has earned your salvation for you, you can have confident assurance of eternal life in heaven.

48

You Have Been Chosen to Bear Fruit

You didn't choose me. I chose you. I appointed you to go and produce lasting fruit, so that the Father will give you whatever you ask for, using my name.

JOHN 15:16

Growing up, I was never what you would call "athletic." Instead of being a jock, I was the kid who always had a list of excuses for why I couldn't participate in gym class each day:

- "My head hurts."
- "My doctor said I need to take it easy for a few weeks."
- "I have an ingrown toenail."
- And so on…

This is probably why the majority of my memories from gym class consist of me sitting along the wall reading comic books and occasionally getting pegged upside the head with an errant dodgeball.

Needless to say, whenever my excuses failed me and I was

forced to participate, I was never the first one picked for either team. More often than not, I was one of the last to be chosen.

Maybe that's why I find it so incredible that Jesus actually picked me to be a part of His team. It clearly wasn't because of anything I've done to earn the spot, but solely because of His love and His Father's grace.

I will admit, there are times when I look at my skill set and conclude that Jesus must have chosen me to be the third-string punter or perhaps the water boy. Sure, He let me onto the team, but the odds of me seeing any playing time are pretty slim.

But that's not the case at all. Jesus chose me so that I could produce lasting fruit. Or, to put it in today's terms, to do stuff that makes a difference in His Kingdom. He wants to pass me the ball so I can score.

And this isn't His special plan for only me either. It's His plan for every single person who has put their faith in Him.

So the next time you feel like you're sitting on the sidelines waiting to be put into the game, remember that Jesus specifically chose you to be a player, not just a benchwarmer. Ask Him what play He wants you to run next, and trust Him to give you the ability to run it.

The best part of all this is, even if you fumble the ball a hundred times, Jesus will never cut you from His team.

49

You Have Been Made Dead to Sin

[Jesus] personally carried our sins in his body on the cross, so that we can be dead to sin and live for what is right. By his wounds you are healed.

I PETER 2:24

In order to comprehend the full depth of what this verse means for us, we first need to remember what is true about those who haven't trusted in Christ:

1. When Adam chose to live his life apart from God, sin entered into mankind and brought with it death. This sin is in the hearts of all mankind from birth.[1]
2. The only way to be set free from the penalty of your sin is for it to be included in the death of Jesus.[2]
3. If you die physically without trusting Jesus to pay the penalty of your sin, the sin in your heart will keep you separated from God for all eternity.

So, instead of being dead to sin, those who are still living independently from Christ are dead *in* their sin. The sin within them defines who they are, dictates how they are able to live, and destines where they will spend eternity.

No matter how you spin it, that is not good news.

But let's look at what this verse says about those of us who *have* trusted in Christ:

1. When Jesus was on the cross, all of your sins (past, present, and future) were placed on His body.
2. When He died, His death fulfilled the penalty of your sin. And now that your sin debt has been satisfied, it will never need to be paid again.
3. When Christ came back to life, you were also included in His everlasting life. This life of Christ within you is what gives you the power to live righteously today.

All that being said, because of Jesus' work on the cross, you are now dead to sin and alive in Christ. Your old identity of sinner was crucified with Jesus, and you were given a new identity as a holy, righteous saint.

But if I'm dead to sin, why do I still struggle with it?

Perhaps the better question is: "How does God view those who are in Christ when they fall back into sin?"

Scripture answers that question clearly:

> Therefore there is now no condemnation for those who are in Christ Jesus (Romans 8:1).

Because of what Christ did for you on the cross, you have been made dead to the *penalty* of your sins. Your sin will never again define how God sees you. In fact, when God looks at you, He sees you as holy and blameless.

Yes, all of us will struggle with sin from time to time...even after we trust Christ. But those struggles no longer define us in the eyes of God.

Furthermore, the life of Christ within you gives you the power you need to walk away from sin. You may not always choose to, but for the first time in your life you actually have the ability to do so.

And that, my friend, is good news.

50

You Can No Longer Be Touched by the Evil One

We know that God's children do not make a practice of sinning, for God's Son holds them securely, and the evil one cannot touch them.

I JOHN 5:18

When I was growing up, I would torment my brother by playing the "I'm not touching you" game. I'd move my finger as close to him as possible without actually making contact. As if that wasn't annoying enough, I would then hold it there for as long as it took to get a reaction from him.

Naturally, he would become irritated and tell me to knock it off. My response, being the brat that I was, was always the same: "Knock what off? I'm not even touching you."

In a lot of ways, this is the same game that Satan plays with you as a believer. The difference, however, is that he doesn't hold back from touching you because he's content with merely annoying you. He holds back from touching you because he no longer has the power to touch you.

He knows this, of course. Which is why he will still try

to get as close to you as possible. He will push up against the force field of faith[1] that surrounds you, leaning in close enough to whisper accusations in your ear to try to deceive you into believing you are still vulnerable.

But these are lies. You are not vulnerable. The evil one cannot touch you.

I encourage you to rest in this verse. Remind yourself of it whenever you face temptation. Believe it is true, even for you. Trust that the shield of faith truly will protect you from the fiery arrows of accusation, condemnation, and temptation that Satan hurls toward you.

Remember, you are in Christ. You are a child of God, a saint, fused with Jesus Himself, secure for all eternity.

Which means, no matter how untrue it may feel at times, you have been made utterly invincible to the attacks of the enemy.

51

You Have a Secure Future

"For I know the plans I have for you," says the Lord. "They are plans for good and not for disaster, to give you a future and a hope."

JEREMIAH 29:11

Chances are, you've at least considered the thought that God had big plans for you once. But not anymore. That ship has sailed.

Maybe it's because of something you did in the past or something that was done to you. Perhaps it's the accumulated effects of all the shame and guilt that come with an addiction or some other sin you can't seem to get over. Either way, you look at the path your life has taken and believe the lie that God can no longer use you.

You must realize that *nothing* from your past will ever be bad enough to disqualify you from the amazing future God has planned for you. Just look at God's words to the Israelites through the prophet Jeremiah.

For the first 28 chapters of the book, God lays out a list of all the ways the Israelites have turned away from Him. There's adultery and idolatry. They've listened to false prophets and allowed paganism to corrupt their worship. The entire nation has hardened their hearts toward God and rejected His ways.

As a consequence for these sins, God has allowed them to be taken into exile by the Babylonians. But even then, He doesn't give up on them.

In the 29th chapter, God encourages His people to not lose heart even while they remain in captivity. He calls them to set their eyes back on Him and warns them to not be deceived again. He encourages them that this period of exile will not last forever and that He hasn't forgotten them.

Then, in the midst of one of the lowest points in Israel's history, God makes this stunning promise to them:

> "I know the plans I have for you," says the Lord. "They are plans for good and not for disaster, to give you a future and a hope" (Jeremiah 29:11).

No matter how far the Israelites strayed from God, they would always be welcomed back into His good plan once they chose to trust Him again. And it's no different with you and me.

Regardless of where you have been, God still has a plan for you.

A plan with a future.

A plan full of hope.

52

You Are an Heir to God's Glory

Since we are his children, we are his heirs. In fact, together with Christ we are heirs of God's glory. But if we are to share his glory, we must also share his suffering.
ROMANS 8:17

Imagine receiving an e-mail one day informing you that you're the last remaining relative of a wealthy king. You have never met this man, but if it turns out to be true, it means you're now the heir to a great fortune. Your financial troubles are over.

Sadly, these e-mails are never true.

But what if there's an even better inheritance set aside for you? One that would put any earthly kingdom to shame? One that would solve more than just your financial troubles?

That, my friend, is true.

The moment you are adopted as a child of God through your union with Jesus, you become an heir to His glory. Your name is written into God's will, right next to Jesus.

It seems rather pointless for God to have a will, though, doesn't it? After all, He is eternal, so why would He need to dictate where His stuff goes after He dies if He's never going to die?

That's why this will is different: It's tied to *your* life, not to God's.

In other words, this will kicks in when *you* die.

But here's where it gets really good: You've already died.

Excuse me?

As one who has trusted Jesus, you've been crucified with Him.[1] The old you is dead. The new you, however, was resurrected with Christ and is currently seated in heaven.[2] Which means you've already received your inheritance.[3]

The riches of God's glory and grace are available to you today.

This is great news, because, as the second half of this verse warns us, life won't always be rainbows and kittens for those who follow Christ. We're going to need God's help to get us through.

But we can trust that He will always give us what we need. Why?

Because He already has.

Conclusion

What's the Point of All This?

Okay, so you're a child of God. You're seated in the heavenlies. You're part of God's royal priesthood. What difference does all that make in your day-to-day life?

To answer that, let me give you an illustration.

Imagine you are walking down a crowded street and everywhere you look you see people scowling back at you. All you hear are whispers of accusation and condemnation. Not only that, but also every alley you walk by is lined with scantily clad beauties offering you illicit affairs and promising you an escape from the noise of the crowd.

Picture this scene while thinking to yourself, *I am a sinner. I'm worthless. Nobody loves me. I am a slave to my sin.*

How do you respond to the accusations? How do you respond to the temptations? You will desperately want to retreat from the fear and pain caused by the verbal assaults of the crowd. When you hear the offer of love and acceptance from the alleys, it will be nearly impossible to resist its pull. You know it's a sin to give in, but you already feel like a failure, so what's one more mistake going to matter? By viewing yourself as a sinner, you have resigned yourself to the fact that you will eventually give in, just as you always do.

Now, picture the same scene again, but this time, think to yourself, *I am in Christ and He is in me. I am a child of God. I am a saint. Sin has no power over me.*

Is your response any different now? I am willing to bet it is. When you view yourself this way, it becomes much easier for you to ignore the condemning voices because you know the things they are saying about you are no longer true. When you understand how much you are loved and accepted by God, you won't feel the need to receive love and acceptance from the illicit back-alley opportunities. When you understand your true identity, it puts your eyes back onto God, His love, and what He says is true about you. It allows you to walk in His power rather than your own.

Understanding your true identity as "in Christ," and all the benefits that come with that, will help you maintain a proper perspective. And in the same way this perspective empowers you to resist the temptations in the previous illustration, it will also empower you to resist the temptations you encounter in real life.

So let me ask you again, who are you?

Are you a sinner? Are you an addict? Not anymore, my friend!

If you have put your hope in Christ, you are a child of God! You are a saint! You are dead to sin!

Try to remind yourself of these truths every day. It's amazing

the difference they will make in your life—and in your journey to freedom from whatever struggles you face in life.

Define yourself radically as one beloved by God.
This is the true self. Every other identity is illusion.
BRENNAN MANNING

Notes

Introduction: Who Do You Think You Are?

1. See Genesis 3.

4: You Are a New Creation

1. If you're interested in reading the full story of my addiction and learning what the Lord taught me about finding freedom, then pick up a copy of my book, *10 Lies Men Believe about Porn*, anywhere books are sold.
2. Ezekiel 36:26
3. 1 Corinthians 6:18–19
4. 1 Corinthians 1:30

5: You Have Become a Child of God

1. www.beltoftruth.com
2. Psalm 127:3

11: You Are Welcome in God's Presence

1. 1 Peter 2:9

13: You Became Part of God's Royal Priesthood

1. 1 Corinthians 7:4

14: You Have Received Wisdom from God

1. http://dictionary.reference.com/browse/wisdom?s=t
2. http://biblehub.com/commentaries/1_corinthians/1-30.htm
3. James 1:5
4. Luke 12:11–12

15: You Were Joined to the Lord

1. Matthew 19:1–6
2. Revelation 2:17

16: You Are No Longer a Slave—You Are a Friend of Jesus

1. See Romans 6:17–23.
2. See Galatians 4:1–7

17: You Have Been Adopted by God

1. Luke 15:11–32

19: You Have Been Washed Clean

1. Romans 3:23

25: You Have the Ability to Be Thankful in All Circumstances

1. Romans 8:28

28: You Have Been Seated in the Heavenly Realms

1. Galatians 2:20

32: You Have Been Set Free from Fear

1. Matthew 6:26
2. John 11:23–26

33: You Have Received Power, Love, and Self-Discipline

1. 1 John 4:19
2. 2 Corinthians 9:8

37: You Have Received All the Riches You Need

1. Luke 16:19–31

40: Your Roots Have Been Planted in Fertile Soil

1. Matthew 13

43: You Have Received the Gifts of Faith

1. Ephesians 2:8

49: You Have Been Made Dead to Sin

1. Romans 5:12
2. Romans 6:7

50: You Can No Longer Be Touched by the Evil One

1. Ephesians 6:16

52: You Are an Heir to God's Glory

1. Galatians 2:20
2. Ephesians 2:6
3. Ephesians 1:3

ABOUT THE AUTHOR

Stephen Kuhn has been writing books, leading recovery groups, speaking at college campuses, and providing free resources and personal coaching through Belt of Truth Ministries since the day his heart was steamrolled by Jesus. His passion is to allow God to use the story of redemption in his life to encourage others to seek healing through the work of Christ as well.

Stephen lives in Oregon with his wife and daughters. Like most native Northwesterners, he enjoys a good rain shower and probably drinks too much coffee. He spends his weekends hiking, climbing, and skiing, but his greatest joy is building epic Lego creations with his family.

To learn more about Stephen's books, read his blog, or find additional resources, please visit him at **www.beltoftruth.com**.

www.ingramcontent.com/pod-product-compliance
Ingram Content Group UK Ltd.
Pitfield, Milton Keynes, MK11 3LW, UK
UKHW021509180625
459791UK00009B/63

9 781478 970736